arcola
theatre

KTR Productions in association with Gúna Nua presents

In Skagway
by Karen Ardiff

In Skagway was first performed at the
Arcola Theatre, London, on 6 February 2014

In Skagway

by Karen Ardiff

Cast

May	**Geraldine Alexander**
Frankie	**Angeline Ball**
T-Belle	**Kathy Rose O'Brien**
Nelly	**Natasha Starkey**

Director	**Russell Bolam**
Designer	**Natasha Piper**
Lighting Designer	**Katharine Williams**
Composition and Sound Design	**George Dennis**
Movement Director	**Lucy Cullingford**
Production Manager	**Andy Reader**
Stage Manager	**Silki Morrison**
Casting Director	**Ruth O'Dowd**
Assistant Director	**Lisa Carroll**
Dialect Coach	**Richard Ryder**
PR	**Chloé Nelkin Consulting**
Producer	**KTR Productions**
Associate Producer	**Emily Slack**

In Skagway was originally commissioned by Gúna Nua Theatre Company and premiered as *The Goddess of Liberty* in February 2012 at the Project Arts Centre, Dublin, produced by Gúna Nua and Civic Theatre, Dublin.

The performance lasts approximately 90 minutes.

There will be no interval.

Cast

May | GERALDINE ALEXANDER

Theatre includes: *Strange Interlude, Pillars of the Community* (National); *Plain Dealer, The Plantagenets* (RSC); *The Welsh Boy* (Ustinov Studio, Bath); *For Once, The Empty Quarter* (Hampstead); *In Praise of Love* (Royal and Derngate, Northampton); *State of Emergency* (Gate, Notting Hill); *Fall* (Traverse, Edinburgh); *The Maids* (Brighton Festival); *I Saw Myself* (Wrestling School, London); *Jude the Obscure, Flesh and Blood* (Method and Madness); *A Streetcar Named Desire* (Mercury, Colchester); *Inconceivable* (West Yorkshire Playhouse); *The Real Thing* (tour); *The Seagull, A Woman of No Importance, Present Laughter, Hamlet* (Royal Exchange, Manchester); *Titus Andronicus, A Midsummer Night's Dream, The Tempest, Two Noble Kinsmen* (Shakespeare's Globe); *Holy Terror* (also on tour); *Sweet Bird of Youth* (West End). Television includes: *Quick Cuts, Shetland, Case Sensitive, Any Human Heart, Law & Order UK, EastEnders, Casualty, Silent Witness, Fatal Passage, Coronation Street, Holby City, Extras, Love Soup, The Government Inspector, Taggart, Dance to the Music of Time, Bomber, Midsomer Murders*. Film includes: *Messages,The Discovery of Heaven, Merchant Garcon, The Wall of Tyranny*. Geraldine wrote and directed *Amygdala* at the Print Room.

Frankie | ANGELINE BALL

Theatre includes: *Greta Garbo Comes to Donegal* (Tricycle); *The Playboy of the Western World* (Abbey and Peacock); *The Plough and the Stars* (Dublin Gaiety); *Rocky Horror Picture Show* (SFX Dublin). Television includes: *Shameless* (Company Productions); *EastEnders* (BBC1); *Doc Martin* (Buffalo Pictures); *Warriors* (Bell Town Films); *What We Did on our Holidays* (Granada Television); *Rose and Maloney, Over the Rainbow* (ITV); *Ulysses* (Stalheim Ltd); *Anytime Now, Our Friends in the North, Casualty* (BBC); *Score* (BBC Wales); *Christmas Carol* (London Weekend Television); *Randall & Hopkirk Deceased* (Working Title); *Peak Practice VIII* (Carlton); *Highlander* (Gaumont Production). Film includes: *Albert Nobbs* (Mockingbird Pictures); *Cold Turkey, Hard Times* (Feature Productions); *Holy Water* (Feature Productions); *Dead Long Enough* (Blu Egg Production); *Tiger's Tale, Bloom* (Stalheim Ltd); *The General* (Red Sword Production); *The Gambler* (Gambler Productions); *Brothers in Trouble* (BBC/Renegade Films); *Two Nudes Bathing* (Painted World Ltd); *My Girl II* (Columbia); *The Commitments* (20th Century Fox); *Bait* (Monogram); *I'll Do Anything* (Columbia); *Ransom* (Sky); *The Mall* (Warner Bros.); *Trojan Eddie* (Cairnda WN Ltd).

T-Belle | KATHY ROSE O'BRIEN

Kathy Rose is a graduate of RADA and has a BA Hons degree in Drama and Theatre Studies from The Samuel Beckett Centre, Trinity College Dublin. Theatre includes: *Bedroom Farce, Hay Fever* (Spoleto Festival USA); *Little Women* (Gate, Dublin); *The Plough and the Stars, The Passing, Alice in Funderland, The Burial at Thebes* (Abbey, Dublin); *Leaves,* for which she received an Irish Times Theatre Award nomination for Best Supporting Actress (Druid Theatre Company and the Royal Court); *Slattery's Sago Saga* (Dublin Theatre Festival, The Performance Corporation); The Rep Experiment: *Mr Kolpert* and *Platonov* (Once Off Productions); *Listening Out ,What's Their Life Got?* (Theatre503); *ANGLO: The Musical* (Verdant); *Captain Oates' Left Sock* (Finborough); *The Birthday Party* (Bristol Old Vic). She played the title roles in *Ellamenope Jones: The Musical* and *The Fall of Herodias Hattigan* (Randloph SD | The Company). She has worked twice award-winning novelist Joseph O'Connor on his play *Handel's Crossing* (Fishamble: The New Play Company) and as Molly Allgood, the heroine of his novel *Ghost Light* at numerous events as part of Dublin's 'One City One Book'. Television includes: *The Whistleblower* (RTÉ); *George Gently* (BBC). Radio includes: *The Burial at Thebes, The Pipes, The Disappeared, Doping Games* (RTÉ). Film includes: *The Legend of Longwood, Wild*. In 2013 Kathy Rose was invited to speak as a panellist at the first World Actors Forum.

Nelly | NATASHA STARKEY

Natasha is a graduate of the New York Conservatory for Dramatic Arts. Since training, Natasha has returned to the UK and has appeared on stage, in independent film and most recently in her first TV role as Crystal Lumsden in Buffalo Pictures' *Doc Martin VI* for ITV. Credits include *Happy Ending* (Orange Tree); *Rescue Me* (Faroutman); *Guest* (Letterbox Films); *Occasional Justice* (Marika D. Litz); *Dr G* (Tony Films Ltd); *Excuses Excuses* (GNH Productions); *The Couch* (Timewarp Productions).

Creative

Writer | KAREN ARDIFF

Karen is an actress living and working in Dublin. She has performed on every major stage in Ireland and has been nominated for the Irish Times Theatre Awards on four occasions, winning Best Actress for *Love in the Title* by Hugh Leonard at the Abbey Theatre. *In Skagway* is her first play and was commissioned by Gúna Nua Theatre Company and produced by Gúna Nua and the Civic Theatre under the title *The Goddess of Liberty*. The play won the Irish Playwrights and Screenwriters Guild Best New Play Award, the Stewart Parker/BBC Northern Ireland Award and was nominated for the Susan Smith Blackburn Prize. Karen is also a novelist. Her first novel *The Secret of my Face* is translated into Chinese and Albanian. She lives in Dublin with Mick and their son Harry.

Director | RUSSELL BOLAM

Russell trained at Middlesex University and GITIS Academy of Theatre Arts, Moscow. Theatre credits include *The Merry Wives of Windsor* (Ivan Vazov Theatre); *The Seagull, Shivered* (Southwark Playhouse); *Somersaults, Captain Oates' Left Sock* (Finborough); *Alfred* (Vineyard Theatre); *The Road to Mecca* (Arcola Theatre); *The Roman Bath* (Arcola/Ivan Vazov); *Three More Sleepless Nights, Fourplay* (Tristan Bates); and *The Physicists* (Aphra Studio). Russell is a visiting director at Central School of Speech and Drama, Royal Welsh College of Music and Drama, Oxford School of Drama, has taught improvisation at Bristol Old Vic Theatre School and is a part-time teacher at Kent University.

Designer | NATASHA PIPER

Natasha trained at Central School of Speech and Drama. She is associate designer for Milk Presents. Designs include: *A Real Man's Guide to Sainthood* – dir. Lucy Doherty (Camden People's Theatre and national tour); *Mad Forest* – dir. Russell Bolam (Embassy); *Daffodil Scissors/Burn* – dir. Lucy Doherty (Berry); *Opera Scenes* – dir. Edward Dick (Guildhall School of Music & Drama); *The Mystery of Edwin Drood* – dir. Matthew Gould (Landor); *The Duchess of Malfi* – dir. Bruce Jamieson (Greenwich Playhouse); *The Golden Dragon* – dir. Ramin Gray (Actors Touring Company).

Lighting Designer | KATHARINE WILLIAMS

Katharine is a lighting designer working in drama, dance and physical theatre, with some opera, musical and circus projects. She works in the UK and internationally. Her designs have been seen in China, Hong Kong, New Zealand, Canada, the USA, Mexico, Ireland, Holland, Spain, Italy, Germany, Armenia, Romania, Russia and the Czech Republic. Credits include: *Moominland Midwinter, Heidi – A Goat's Tale, Landscape & Monologue , The French Detective and the Blue Dog* (Theatre Royal Bath); *Billy the Girl* (Clean Break); *The Noise* (Unlimited Theatre); *The Ruling Class* (English Theatre, Frankfurt); *A Midsummer Night's Dream, Cyrano de Bergerac, Othello* (Grosvenor Park Open Air Theatre); *Address Unknown* (Soho); *Not I, The Westbridge* (Royal Court); *Say It With Flowers* (Sherman Cymru); *Resonance at the Still Point of Change* (Southbank Centre); *Ballroom of Joy and Sorrows* (Watford Palace); *Krapps Last Tape / Spoonface Steinberg* (Hull Truck); *Anne and Zef* (Company of Angels); *God/Head* (Chris Goode and Company); *Invisible* (Transport Theatre); *The Pajama Men* (Assembly); *Closer* (Théâtre des Capucins); *Faeries* (Royal Opera House); *Ivan and the Dogs* (ATC/Soho); *The Goat, Or Who Is Sylvia?* (Traverse, Edinburgh); *Reykjavic* (Shams); *Nocturnal* (Gate); *Amgen: Broken* (Sherman Cymru/Theatr Clywd); *Dolls* (National Theatre of Scotland); *I Am Falling* (Gate Theatre/Sadler's Wells); *Touched... for the Very First Time* (Trafalgar Studios).

Composition and Sound Design | GEORGE DENNIS

Theatre includes: *The Island* (Young Vic); *Love Your Soldiers* (Sheffield Crucible Studio); *The Love-Girl and the Innocent, The Seagull, The Only True History of Lizzie Finn, Someone Who'll Watch Over Me, Antigone* (Southwark Playhouse); *The Last Yankee* (Print Room); *Dances of Death* (Gate); *Thark* (Park Theatre); *Carnival of the Animals, The York Realist* (Riverside Studios); *Moth* (HighTide Festival/Bush); *Beautiful Thing* (Arts/UK tour); *Hello/Goodbye* (Hampstead Downstairs); *Liar Liar* (Unicorn); *Good Grief* (Theatre Royal Bath/UK tour); *The Seven Year Itch* (Salisbury Playhouse); *The Living Room, Bloody Poetry* (Jermyn Street); *A Life, The Drawer Boy, Foxfinder, The Goodnight Bird, The Captive, Me and Juliet, Generous* (Finborough); *Shiverman* (Theatre503); *When Did You Last See My Mother?* (Trafalgar Studios 2); *Unrestless* (Old Vic Tunnels).

Production Manager | ANDY READER

Andy is a production manager for theatre, dance, circus and live events. He is technical manager of the annual Dancin' Oxford Festival, associate production manager for Cirque Bijou, and technical director of Unfinished Productions. Recent work includes: *Our Big Land* (New Wolsey and tour); *Lizzie Siddal* (Arcola); *The Lion, the Witch and the Wardrobe, Aladdin* (North Wall); *Henry V, Cette Immense Intimité, Danses Des Cariatides, Traverse* (Oxford Castle); *The Aeneid, Lord of the Flies* (Oxford Playhouse).

Movement Director | LUCY CULLINGFORD

Recent productions include: *The Spanish Golden Age Season* (Ustinov, Bath, and Arcola); *A Season in the Congo* (Young Vic); *The Double* (Ustinov, Bath); *Constellations* (Royal Court and Duke of York's); *The Revenger's Tragedy* (Hoxton Hall); *Matilda The Musical, Dance Repetiteur* (RSC/Cambridge); *Lives in Art* (Crucible, Sheffield); *Yerma* (Hull Truck and the Gate); *The Phoenix of Madrid* (Ustinov Studio, Bath); *Othello* (Rose, Kingston); *Quartet* (Old Vic Tunnels); *Happy Days* (Crucible Studio, Sheffield); *Bed and Sofa, Beating Heart Cadaver* (Finborough); *The Winter's Tale, Macbeth* (Custom Practice); *Gotcha* (Riverside Studios). As Movement Assistant: *The Grain Store, The Drunks* (RSC, Courtyard Theatre); *A Tender Thing* (RSC/Northern Stage); *The Winter's Tale, A Midsummer Night's Dream,* RSC Youth Ensemble (Courtyard); *The Great British Country Fête* (Bush); *Not for All the Tea in China* (Chol); *A Doll's House, A Christmas Carol* (Bridge House, Warwick); *Stoopud Fucken Animals* (Traverse, Edinburgh); *A Small Family Business* (West Yorkshire Playhouse); *Grace Online, No Stone Unturned* (Youth Music Theatre UK); *Mikey the Pikey* (Pleasance, Edinburgh); *A Christmas Cracker, Moby Dick, Pigs, Big Trouble in the Little Bedroom, Thick As A Brick, Bouncers* (Hull Truck). Lucy worked as a movement practitioner in the Movement Department of the Royal Shakespeare Company for two years, working on David Farr's *The Winter's Tale,* Greg Doran's *Hamlet, Love's Labour's Lost* and *A Midsummer Night's Dream* (Courtyard). Lucy is currently Dance Repetiteur for the RSC's production *Matilda.* In 2010 she was RSC/Warwick University Creative Fellow in Residence, where she directed *The Renaissance Body,* performed as part of the reopening of the Swan Theatre, Stratford. Lucy regularly leads workshops for theatre companies, universities and drama schools. She currently teaches movement at ALRA and Mountview Academy of Theatre Arts, and has previously taught at ArtsEd, Rose Bruford and Central School of Speech and Drama.

Assistant Director | LISA CARROLL

Lisa undertook the Foundation Course at RADA and recently graduated from University College Dublin. Theatre credits include: *Three Cities* (Edinburgh Fringe Festival); *Breathing Corpses* (University College, Dublin, Granary Theatre, Cork); *Terminus* (University College, Dublin, Firkin Crane, Cork); *A Couple of Poor, Polish Speaking Romanians* (University College, Dublin, Belltable Arts Centre, Limerick); *The Pain and the Itch* (University College, Dublin). As assistant director: *Green Street* (Gúna Nua/Percolate).

Associate Producer | EMILY SLACK

Emily has produced work for the Theatre Royal Bury St Edmunds, Bury Festival and The Production Exchange. She is also Associate Producer for Real Circumstance Theatre Company, for whom she produced the tour and London premiere of *Our Share of Tomorrow* at Theatre503 in 2013. Emily has also worked for BBC Drama, Just Casting and Hoxton Street Management. Projects include: *Aladdin, Romeo and Juliet, Rapunzel and the Rascal Prince, Mansfield Park* (national tour), and rehearsed readings including: *School for Arrogance, Miss in her Teens, Who's the Dupe, Speed the Plough, Lovers' Vows* and *A Bold Stroke for a Wife* (Theatre Royal Bury St Edmunds); *Ramble with the Romantics* (Theatre Royal Bury St Edmunds and Bury Festival); *Our Share of Tomorrow* (Real Circumstance Theatre Company, tour and Theatre503); *The Pearl, Emily – The Making of a Militant Suffragette* (The Production Exchange, national tour).

Stage Manager | SILKI MORRISON

Theatre credits include: *In Skagway* – dir. Russell Bolam (Arcola); *Phoenix* – dir. Maggie Norris (Hackney Studios); *Holes* by Tom Basden (Invisible Dot/Assembly); *Threeway* – dir. Phillip Breen (Invisible Dot/Pleasance); *Moth* by Declan Greene (HighTide/Bush); *Bottleneck* by Luke Barnes (Hightide/Pleasance); *I Heart Peterborough* by Joel Horwood (Assembly/Soho); *Les Mammelles de Tiresias Opera* (Aldeburgh Music, Jubilee Hall); *Eisteddfod* by Luke Barnes, *Incoming* by Andrew Motion (HighTide/Latitude); *Margaret Catchpole* (Eastern Angles/Hush House); *Clockwork* by Laura Poliakoff (HighTide); *Little Upper Downing Tour* (Little Bulb/Farnham Maltings); *Round the Twist* (Sir John Mills/Seckford); *Pinocchio* (Jubilee Hall); *Dusk Rings a Bell* by Stephen Belber (HighTide/Assemby/Watford Palace); *Midnight Your Time* – dir. Michael Longhurst, with Diana Quick (HighTide/Assembly); *Twelfth Night* (RRC); *Kabaddi, Kabaddi, Kabaddi* by Satinder Chohan (Salisbury/Kali); *Bentwater Roads* by Tony Ramsey (Eastern Angles/The Hush House); *Mansfield Park* (Eastern Angles/Seckford); *Lincoln Road* – dir. Naomi Jones. Television and film credits include: BBC and ITV documentaries and commercials (Producer, Bruizer Productions); Franz Ferdinand, The Killers, The Stereophonics, Kula Shaker, McFly, Soulsavers, The Noisettes (Collision Films); Vodafone commercials (Aardman Animations). Production co-ordinator on *The Rapture* with Danny Dyer and Jaime Murray. Events include: Roots Manuva, The Correspondents, Playfest, Tim Key (Assembly), Big Top/Main Stage – Bestival, Latitude, Green Man Festivals.

Dialect Coach | RICHARD RYDER

Richard Ryder has worked in the voice department of the RSC and is currently a member of the national Theatre voice department. With his company, The Big Gob Squad, February 2014 sees 'The Accent Kit' (an accent app for actors) released for iPhone. For the Arcola: *Road to Mecca, but i cd only whisper, Moby Dick, In Skagway*. Other theatre includes: *A Taste of Honey, Blurred Lines, Protest Song, 50 Years on Stage, Emil and the Detectives, Home, Romeo and Juliet, Table, This House, Port, The Captain of Köpenick, Cocktail Sticks, Hymn* (National); *Untold Stories* (National/West End); *The Tempest, The Merchant of Venice* (RSC); *American Psycho, The Turn of the Screw* (Almeida); *Oh! What a Lovely War* (Theatre Royal Stratford East); *It Just Stopped* (Orange Tree); *Paper Dolls, Red Velvet* (Tricycle); *The Duck House* (Vaudeville/tour); *Barking in Essex* (Wyndham's); *Race, Hysteria* (Hampstead); *Proof* (Menier Chocolate Factory); *The Winslow Boy* (Old Vic); *One Monkey Don't Stop No Show* (Eclipse); *Uncle Vanya* (Vaudeville); *The Thirty-Nine Steps* (West End/tour); *Oliver!, The History Boys, My Fair Lady, A Taste of Honey* (Crucible, Sheffield); *The Kingdom* (Soho); *Beautiful Burnout* (Frantic Assembly); *The Norman Conquests* (Liverpool Everyman); *Twist of Gold* (Polka); *Wonderful Town* (Manchester Royal Exchange). www.therichervoice.com and www.thebiggobsquad.com

KTR Productions

KTR Productions is a UK grown company creating theatre and film from their offices in North Yorkshire, England. KTR seeks to innovate and prides itself on integrating both established and unknown talent into its team on a bespoke project-to-project basis, as well as championing 'the north' as a legitimate territory within which to base the company. KTR's commitment to operating slightly outside of the parameters of common practice ensures that there is always an exciting mix of perspectives and a more invigorating process by which KTR loves to work.

Creating opportunities is KTR's driving force and KTR has been proudly 'making things happen' since 2013.

KTR wishes to thank the following companies and individuals for their generous support and patronage, without which the British Premiere of *In Skagway* would have not been possible this February/March 2014. KTR Productions is forever in their debt.

Companies
Neo G Ltd
Responsible Life Ltd
Affinia Partnerships
Buffalo Pictures
Gúna Nua Theatre Company
Chloe Nelkin Consulting
Guildhall School of Music and Drama
Central School of Speech and Drama

Individuals
Paul Starkey
Fred Starkey
Steve Wilkie
Mila Starkey
Alexandra Jones
Dan Jones
Alan Trewhitt
Carmen del Prado
Angie Capol
Chris Hislop
Paul Meade
Leyla Nazli
Maree Kearns
Aurora Wilson
Victor Kay

Gúna Nua Theatre Company

'One of Ireland's most original, even radical, companies'
Sunday Times

Gúna Nua Theatre is an independent theatre production
company based in Dublin, Ireland. The company has a
strong commitment to devising and producing new Irish
writing and presenting radical interpretations of classic
plays. It has established a reputation for innovative, vital and
exciting theatre that has received an overwhelmingly
positive response from audiences and critics alike. Founded
in 1998 by Paul Meade and David Parnell, Gúna Nua has
produced 21 shows, 14 of them new plays by Irish writers and
received numerous awards and nominations for its work:
Scenes from a Watercooler (Best Production Dublin Fringe
2001), *Skin Deep* (Stewart Parker Award for Best New Play
2004), *Little Gem* (Carol Tambor Best of Edinburgh Award,
BBC/Stewart Parker Radio Drama Award, Fishamble/Fringe
Best New Play Award, Irish Playwrights and Screenwriters
Guild Best New Play 2008–11), *The Goddess of Liberty*
(BBC/Stewart Parker Radio Drama Award and Irish
Playwrights and Screenwriters Guild Best New Play 2013),
Pondling (Best Female Performer Dublin Fringe 2013.)

Gúna Nua is grant aided by the Arts Council, Dublin City
Council and Culture Ireland and has toured extensively
around Ireland as well as to Britain, Australia, Europe and
the US.

Arcola Theatre

Since 2001, Arcola Theatre has taken thousands of theatergoers on a theatrical journey by producing and presenting some of the most diverse and challenging work for the London stage. We have presented plays, operas and musicals that have rarely seen the light of day as well as revisiting more contemporary playwrights and presenting the finest international work. Arcola has championed new writers and emerging directors by offering them a platform on which to continue their journey.

For Arcola Theatre

Artistic Director	**Mehmet Ergen**
Executive Producer	**Leyla Nazli**
Executive Director	**Ben Todd**
General Manager	**Jamie Arden**
Technical Manager	**Geoff Hense**
Engagement Manager	**Nick Connaughton**
Commercial Manager	**Ruth Tosha Mulandi**
Front of House Manager	**Charlotte Croft**
Sustainability Projects Manager	**Feimatta Conteh**
Marketing Assistant	**Catherine Veitch**
Duty Managers	**Amelia Hankin, Miriam Mahony**
Bar Supervisors	**Oya Bacak, Cassie Leon, Seth Petherick**
Casual Staff, Interns and Volunteers	Thanks to our Ushers, Bar Staff, and Volunteers and Work Placement Students, whose contributions are invaluable.

The Arcola Bar offers a daily menu of classic Southern Mediterranean dishes by El Molino, home-made sandwiches, salads and cakes, and a selection of locally sourced, organic wines, beers, spirits, coffees and teas. Interval drinks and refreshments – including handmade ice creams – can be pre-odered.

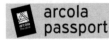 **arcola passport**

- Love Arcola Theatre?
- Come often?
- Get the Arcola Passport

- 5 plays for £50 guaranteed
- 10% off at the Arcola Bar
- Valid for up to 12 months

www.arcolatheatre.com | www.facebook.com/Arcola.Theatre | @arcolatheatre

Arcola gratefully acknowledges the ongoing support of

ARTS COUNCIL ENGLAND
LOTTERY FUNDED
Supported using public funding by

Bloomberg   Esmée Fairbairn FOUNDATION   Hackney   THE PRINCE'S FOUNDATION FOR CHILDREN AND THE ARTS   WL

IN SKAGWAY

Karen Ardiff

Characters

FRANKIE, *Frances Harmon, late teens to early sixties*

MAY O'CONNELL, *late teens to early sixties*

T-BELLE O'CONNELL, *May's daughter, thirties*

NELLY THE PIG, *twenties*

Author's Note

Frankie's character has had a stroke and is hemiplegic, and unable to speak or process words for the 'real-time' sections of the play. It is important that the actress plays 'within' the stroke. Frankie may have deficits and altered realities – she may zone out or misconstrue – but she plays her own 'arc' within the real-time scenes, it is just a very different shape from the other characters. I would also resist the temptation to play her with a dropped mouth.

This text went to press before the end of rehearsals and so may differ slightly from the play as performed.

Scene One

*1898. The space is lit to suggest a mean cabin in Skagway,
Alaska. It should not be fully enclosed, to allow side lighting for
the scenes in the past, and should contain uprights with
washing/sacking/netting hanging from them that can be lit to
suggest ships' sails, theatre curtains and lace structures.*

*'Song of the Klondike' by George J. Becker and Nellie V. Millar
(1897) plays, a crackly, old recording.*

> To Alaska to the Klondike we will go
> With pickaxe and shovel we will hoe
> The mines are reeking with golden ore
> New fields we should travel to explore.
> Where cold winds whistle among the hills
> We will settle to work with drills, drills, drills.
>
> CHORUS
> Search the ground for gold, gold, gold.
> While the air is cold, cold, cold.
> Luck will come to the bold, bold, bold.
> Wrongdoers are the ones sold, sold, sold.

*The sounds of a violent wind outside and the stove/wood
crackling rises to drown out the sound of the music.*

*Towards evening. Through this scene, dusk settles into a dark
night.*

MAY *is tending to* FRANKIE *by the light of a single oil lamp
and a small stove, washing her tenderly with a flannel and
warm water from a basin.* FRANKIE *is in a makeshift chair
with wheels, though this is not obvious because of a flannel
draped over the back wheel.*

FRANKIE *seems vaguely troubled, but responds instinctively to*
MAY*'s touch.* MAY *first washes* FRANKIE*'s face –* FRANKIE
moving under MAY*'s hand as if she cannot see.* MAY *next
washes* FRANKIE*'s left hand, playing with it and raising a*

brief smile from FRANKIE, *then she washes her right hand,
which the audience can now see is completely paralysed,
clawed inwards. As* MAY *moves away,* FRANKIE *slumps a
little and* MAY *rights her. It is obvious that* FRANKIE *is
completely paralysed through her right side.* MAY *murmurs to*
FRANKIE *encouragingly as she works.* MAY *is in top form:
what seems from the outside to be a scene of squalor and
despair is to her a scene involving huge strides forward of
progress with* FRANKIE.

MAY *finishes and stands back a little from* FRANKIE. FRANKIE
*is distressed and seems to want something. When she vocalises we
realise that the stroke has robbed her of language also.*

FRANKIE (*pointing and vocalising, but impossible to decipher.
The actress will find her own style of vocalisation, but it is
without meaningful content, repetitive and undifferentiated.*
FRANKIE *has no idea that it does not express what she
believes she is saying*). Wuh whu woooh wooh wooh wooh
wooh. WOOH WUH WUH!!

*She gives up with an imperially dismissive gesture – 'Christ
you people are so fucking stupid!' – and* MAY *washes her
again, regarding her with something akin to despair.*
FRANKIE *sinks into a trance, 'switching off' as if a literal
switch has been pulled.*

MAY *feels* FRANKIE's 'bad' hand – it's cold, so she leans
her forward and settles a shawl around her. It is awkward,
but we see that* MAY *has accustomed herself to 'work' with*
FRANKIE's hemiplegia. FRANKIE *switches back on.*

MAY. Now. That's it, Frances! Up and under. (*Threads the
shawl over* FRANKIE's bad, clawed hand.) Hah! It's just
like old times! 'Cept this time I haven't got my foot in your
poor old back! Huh? Like when I used to tighten your stays?

(*Pantomiming for* FRANKIE, *her foot on the side of the bath
chair as if tightening a woman's corset: exaggerated effort.*) A
haon! A dó! A trí! Brace yourself, Frances!!! Hhnnnnngggh!

FRANKIE *delightedly vocalises along with her, unwittingly
sounding similar – 'HHHHnnnnnggggh!' – and, delighted
with the fun of it all, breaks into hysterical laughter.*

Oh, we had you beautiful for every single performance, didn't we, *a chroí*? (*Exaggerated Dubbelin accent.*) 'Bee-You-Tee-Full' – as you used to say! Because You. Were. The. Show! Yes you were! I was your 'makin'-upper' and you were the show! America's Irish Pride. Mrs O'Diva! Yes you were!

MAY *goes to a wooden trunk downstage, and removes from it lace and lace bobbins, reverentially taking from the bottom of the trunk a little music box. She brings it to* FRANKIE *and holds it out in front of her eyes.*

Remember this, my Frankie? The Goddess of Liberty!

FRANKIE *does not register the music box. Carefully,* MAY *opens the box and a little Statue of Liberty made of lace pops up, with a tiny figure that revolves to a slow Chinese tune that plays on the mechanism inside.* FRANKIE *focuses on the revolving figure and a childlike smile breaks out across her face, huge, echoed by the delight of* MAY.

That's you dancing, Frankie. You delighting them all under your lace canopy, my darling! Made especially in your honour, darling girl.

Look at you. Turning your head twisty-ways the way you drove the men wild! The poor weak feckers! Isn't that it, Frankie? The poor eejits, sure you'll drive them crazy again just as soon as you're better, my own. Won't you not, Frankie?

As the tune and the revolving slow, FRANKIE, *mesmerised by the turning figure, reaches out her good hand very slowly to touch the figure. Her touch makes the music mechanism grind to a halt and sound discordantly.*

There is a sudden sound of a fumbling at the latch of the door. MAY *throws a protective arm around* FRANKIE, *and thrusts the music box under the chair.*

The door is flung open, and there is a sudden sound of a violent gust of air and a flurry of snow before the door is slammed shut by T-BELLE. *She is muffled up so that only her eyes are visible, wearing most of her clothes and carrying a rucksack strung with boots, a pot, some snowshoes, a gunpowder pouch, a gun. She is frozen and wild-eyed, and*

*she shrugs off her pack before rushing to the stove and
hogging it for warmth. She looks over her shoulder to stare at*
FRANKIE *for a bit, but for the moment says nothing.*

T-Belle!

T-BELLE. How long has she been like this?

MAY. I thought you were lost. You weren't at the claim, you
weren't anywhere.

Beat.

I paid our very last… of the day-to-day money… to young
James Ferren to go up looking for you and you weren't
anywhere. Nobody could tell him where you were. Three
weeks after it happened we were still looking for you. James
Ferren couldn't find you on the whole Chilkoot Pass. Four
times he went up there looking for you.

T-BELLE (*deliberately busying herself*). Maybe he took your
'very last' and bought himself some ease and relief at the
Nugget Saloon.

MAY. I trust him.

T-BELLE. More fool you.

Beat.

Well, he found me in the end.

MAY. Nobody else heard him, did they, Tee?

T-BELLE. What's it to you?

MAY. They can't know, T-Belle! Nobody can know that she's…
(*Whispered because of* FRANKIE.) recuperating.

T-BELLE. Well, you needn't worry. I was – (*A panicked
thought.*) How many strangers have been poking round here
while I've been gone?

MAY. No one, Tee. It's private. No one has been here except the
doctor –

T-BELLE. Doctor? What doctor? Ferren, and a doctor? Christ!

MAY. Language, T-Belle!

T-BELLE *goes to a floorboard and pulls it up. There are three sewn-up sacking tubes inside. She feels the weight of them and is relieved. She puts them back and returns to the stove.*

T-BELLE *winds the cloth from around her face and turns once more to regard* FRANKIE. FRANKIE *suddenly has an 'AH!' moment and recognises* T-BELLE. *She vocalises excitedly, pointing her one good hand at* T-BELLE *and then looking to* MAY.

(*Encouraging her.*) Yes! Yes! It's T-Belle! Yes it is! Clever girl!

FRANKIE *continues to vocalise – without any meaning – until she loses interest and lapses into her neutral state.* T-BELLE *is horrified.*

Beat.

(*Miming washing for* FRANKIE, *who nods and smiles in 'understanding'.*) We just had a nice wash.

T-BELLE. Jesus.

MAY *lets the blasphemy go this time.*

MAY. And she's very happy to be all nice and clean to see you, T-Belle! Did you see how well she recognises you? She's a clever thing, yes you are!

T-BELLE (*factual*). She's an imbecile.

MAY (*covers* FRANKIE*'s ears, which distresses* FRANKIE, *who has not understood* T-BELLE*'s comment*). SSSSH! For God's sake, child! You'll upset her!

T-BELLE. Is she going to die?

MAY (*moving up close to* T-BELLE, *sotto voce*). Shut your mouth! Shut your mean mouth! Don't you go upsetting her. We've been doing fine without you.

She returns to FRANKIE.

Don't you mind now, Frankie, that old meanie-pants. She's just cold and she's in a fierce temper from it. (*Mimes to* FRANKIE *a cross face as she says:*) A FIERCE temper!

FRANKIE *laughs fulsomely and briefly, then abruptly switches off. The effect is disturbing.*

That's it now!

T-BELLE. Mamma.

MAY. Like Dr Fenniman said: 'She's had a bad old knock-out for a lady of her age, but sure it won't knock a feather out of a Grande Dame like her I shouldn't wonder!' No indeed it won't, says I, 'No indeed,' said Dr Fenniman.

T-BELLE. I didn't think we had a doctor in Skagway.

MAY. Well! It's funny she should say that! Isn't it, Frankie? We had no idea. But when Frankie took ill, well, this Dr Fenniman had heard of her out east. He had! And he's just a claims man himself, runs a few mines up by the White Pass, so he doesn't need to do any surgery.

T-BELLE. Mamma! Get on with –

MAY. Lord, Frankie! I do ramble on! Well, T-Belle, do you know? Could you possibly guess! He had a cousin of his wife – she's dead now, God rest her – had seen Frankie in *A Winter's Tale*. (*To* FRANKIE.) Seen my darling in Ford's Theatre in Washington. In her greatest triumph. And he said his wife's cousin had talked about it from that day until the day his wife died. They lost touch after that. They weren't close apart from the wife apparently.

T-BELLE. Mamma!

MAY. Oh yes. The cousin said he'd remember to his dying day Frances Harmon as the statue of Hermione the Queen coming to life after twenty long years *frozen*, '*fruzz!*' Isn't that what your mammy used to say, Frankie? The tears running down her cheeks, making the white paint drip off her face. He never forgot it apparently.

T-BELLE. What did the doctor –

MAY. And don't you forget, T-Belle – she started off as a *nothing* in that play. As Mopsa – a peasant girl! With only a handful of lines and a biteen of a song. And she… worked her way up.

T-BELLE. I don't doubt it.

They both look to FRANKIE, *who shudders through her 'good' side and lapses once more into her switched-off state. Stock-still.*

Jesus. What *is that*?

MAY. 'Little jolts', Dr Fenniman said. Just little jolts. Maybe little bits and pieces coming back to her is what I think.

FRANKIE *shudders, switching on again and coming back to the room.*

T-BELLE. I'm hungry.

MAY. You'll have to wait. It'll be tomorrow. James Ferren – The one you said was not reliable! – he's bringing us something tomorrow he says. He's been marvellous so he has. Frankie has a bird's appetite.

T-BELLE. Well, if you're talking about liquor, yes. A gannet.

MAY. How dare you! Frankie doesn't drink.

T-BELLE looks to FRANKIE.

Not since her turn. She hasn't touched a drop.

T-BELLE. Isn't she great.

MAY. We'll ignore that.

Beat.

It's been a shock.

T-BELLE. I'd say it has.

MAY. For you. For you, I mean.

T-BELLE. Well. Yes, Mamma. It's a shock.

Beat.

She's gone.

MAY *takes* T-BELLE *urgently away from* FRANKIE *and talks to her, constantly checking over her shoulder to see that* FRANKIE *is alright.*

MAY. She's not gone. She's not. She's not, T-Belle. Or… If she's a bit 'away', well, we'll get her back.

Beat.

We have to.

T-BELLE. Oh, Mamma.

MAY (*anxiously looking over her shoulder – a whisper*). We have days only and that's all there is about it.

Beat.

It's tight enough I'll admit.

T-BELLE (*takes* MAY*'s hand, awkwardly*). Oh, May. I'm sorry.

MAY (*shrugging herself loose*). It's not pity we need now. We have to get busy. There's so much time wasted already. We couldn't find you. You weren't at the claim. James Ferren asked every miner, tramp and Indian and there was nothing. Where were you, T-Belle? I thought you were dead.

T-BELLE. I was scouting. Further up the pass. With… an Indian who knows the territory. What does it matter?

MAY. Well, you're back now.

T-BELLE. Yes. I'm back.

MAY. And what I think we should do now, T-Belle, is just knuckle down and get her right for the spring.

T-BELLE. For the spring?

MAY. We'll have to muddle through the winter, we can maybe put it off that long, but we'll manage somehow and then it'll be all worthwhile.

T-BELLE. We can't stay here.

MAY. We most certainly can, Theresa-Belle O'Connell! We most certainly can!

T-BELLE. Nobody is staying in Skagway.

MAY. We are.

T-BELLE. No!

Beat.

It's over, Mamma. This whole place is old news. The miners will come down before the pass freezes over and this whole godforsaken mud-bucket town will pile onto the boats and leave. *There's no more gold.* The seams are through. There hasn't been a strike in months. Skagway is over. Any fool stays the winter will starve.

MAY. Soapy Smith bought a dance from Nelly the Pig just over a month ago with a string of gold she could put around her waist! It was the talk of the town. This place is heaving with gold.

T-BELLE. Soapy Smith was shot dead.

MAY. That's a lie.

T-BELLE. He's dead. Got himself shot to death on the jetty. You're only two miles from Main Street, Mamma, how in hell did you not hear?

MAY. Language, T-Belle!

T-BELLE. There'll *be* no spring here. We have to take our gold and go.

MAY. And when were you going to tell us all this? When were you going to walk back down the pass and *inform* us of this calamity?

T-BELLE. We'll find a doctor in Seattle. We'll get her comfortable for her last few months.

MAY. When she gets better we will.

T-BELLE. *Mamma. (Losing patience and returning to the loose board to extract the sacking parcels.)* Tomorrow morning I am going down to Jed Emmerson in the telegraph office and I am going to pay passage for us on the next good boat out of here. In a week's time there won't be room on a safe boat.

MAY. I never heard a thing, T-Belle. I'm sure it's all my eye. We'll stay put. Won't we, pet? *We'll Stay Put!!!*

She mimes staying put. FRANKIE *is puzzled.*

Beat.

We'll have to.

T-BELLE (*still holding one of the sacking tubes, weary*). I'm not going to fight you, Mamma. I'm going down there tomorrow and I'm buying passage and let the few fools battle through the winter with their little stashes.

MAY. You have enough for passage?

T-BELLE. We have plenty, Mamma. We have plenty. But this is all we'll ever take out of Skagway.

MAY *gives a reassuring smile to* FRANKIE, *and then with a worried look takes* T-BELLE *aside again. She pulls at the string at the top of the sacking and grey rocks fall from it to the floor.*

Where is it? *Where!!!*

MAY. It's safe. It's invested. It's safe.

T-BELLE. The other ones? *Are they all –*

MAY. You have to trust me, T-Belle.

T-BELLE. Please do not tell me it's all gone. Please do not tell me you've 'invested' five thousand dollars of gold.

MAY *is silent.*

Answer me.

Beat.

MAY. When the fire happened. You remember the fire?

T-BELLE. Of course I do.

MAY. It razed the town almost. Soapy Smith came over. Jed Emmerson needed cash to rebuild the Nugget and the Criterion. Frankie had mentioned the good fortune that we… I mean you had with that claim –

T-BELLE. She *told* Soapy about – JESUS!

MAY. Your Auntie Frankie is a SHREWD BUSINESSWOMAN!

T-BELLE (*falling to her knees*). Oh my God.

MAY. She gave him the money. AND BEFORE YOU START OFF ON ME I can tell you that we are getting every dime back and *double*.

T-BELLE (*faintly*).When?

MAY. When Frankie dances for the town.

    T-BELLE *stares at her.*

    It was Soapy's idea. He'd been there, you see. He was there. He'd seen her dancing at the opening of the Statue of Liberty, leading the pageant. Of all the actresses and dancers they could have chosen to perform, who did they choose, T-Belle? Who?

T-BELLE. The only actress in America famous for being a lump of rock.

MAY. He had never been more moved he told me. He told Jed all about it and he said, 'Now that would be something, wouldn't it, Jed? And here's the Goddess of Liberty herself come to our Skagway. That would be a thing the town would pay good money to see. If they could see what I saw fifteen years ago they would throw their dollars at the stage – what am I saying? They would throw strings of nuggets at her.'

    And that is what is going to happen in three days' time, T-Belle. Your Auntie Frankie is going to perform the Goddess of Liberty dance in a great lace Statue of Liberty at the opening of the new Criterion Theatre.

T-BELLE (*takes bottle of liquor from her bag*). I think my throat is closing over.

MAY. Do you know what Soapy said: 'I am going to take this money, little lady, and I'm going to build you a stage worthy of your talent.' Didn't he, Frankie? And that's what he has done. It's down there plain for all to see. The New Criterion, due to open in three days' time. And when the dance is over, Jed Emmerson is going to walk out on that stage and give her *six* pokes of gold – *in front of everyone* – and he's going

to say – 'Ladies and gentlemen! I give you the famous
Frances Harmon – the woman who saved the Criterion!'

Beat.

And that's how it's going to be.

Beat.

When we get her back.

T-BELLE. Three days' time?

MAY. Three days' time.

Beat.

But I can see now that maybe it would be better to
postpone –

T-BELLE. They've conned you.

MAY. They have *not* conned us. We have their word of honour.
And I have seen the Statue of Liberty with my own eyes with
lights rigged up inside of it.

T-BELLE. She's given our fortune to a couple of con men so
she can star in her own goddamned *freak show*!

MAY. I will not have you talk like that in front of her! She
knows exactly what she is doing and Jed and Soapy, God rest
him, have the utmost respect for her. Had. Soapy I mean.

T-BELLE. Get it back.

MAY (*quietly*). We can't.

T-BELLE. *Get it back!*

Beat.

MAY. You're not a businesswoman, T-Belle. Your Auntie
Frankie signed a paper. A legal paper. When she dances
they'll give us back the investment and double. Jed was very
clear on that. She knows *exactly* what she's doing.

She points to FRANKIE, *who has slid perilously far down in
the chair.* MAY *goes to right her.*

T-BELLE. Well, let's see, Mamma. You're very tired. I'll go down tomorrow and talk to Jed and maybe we can get one of the Criterion girls to take her place. We'll work something out, Mamma.

MAY. Take her place? Are you quite mad, T-Belle? How could one of those girls take the place of our Frankie? Is Skagway crawling with famous Hermiones? Do they have known tragediennes selling dances at the Monte Carlo bar? This is a moment of history. Nobody could take her place!

T-BELLE. You're tired, Mamma. You're not thinking clearly. Go and lie down for a bit. I'll… sit with her. Go on. I'll wake you in a bit.

MAY. Don't you upset her.

T-BELLE. I won't. I promise.

MAY (*going to the bed in the alcove*). You're too pale. It's not attractive.

T-BELLE (*stung*). Lie down for a bit.

MAY *leaves*. T-BELLE *gathers up the rocks and puts them back in the poke, which she replaces under the floorboard. Then she goes to* FRANKIE *and kneels in front of her, looking straight into her face.*

(*Fiercely.*) Pathetic, isn't it? Isn't it pathetic how she thinks one *slut* couldn't replace another? And you know maybe you can do it! If we just tipped you out it mightn't be so very different from the drunken lurchings you fooled the crowds with fifteen years ago. So tastefully lit under the lace you were. They couldn't see your old ravaged body. Just what they were told. The Famous Actress Frances Harmon recreating her decades-old *turn* of a statue coming to life. Old ham.

I hate you. I hate you so bad it's like a stone *here*. (*Her chest.*) Now we all have to feel sorry for you and spend the rest of our lives changing your drawers and doing your bidding like we've always had to do. Dead like always.

I've spent these last months alive.

Joe made me alive. *My* man. He singled me out. Tlingit Joe.

I heard eagles calling on the mountain. (*Makes a fair imitation of a bird of prey.*) I was shocked like it was a strange thing. It was just so fresh and clear up there they sounded like metal.

What was that? I said. 'Eagles,' he said. 'They're rising on the wind. They're searching.'

Oh! I can see them! Those bright wings! I can see them! and I laughed. I laughed and I fell back into the snow and he laughed and he dived right onto me like he should and he nuzzled his hairless chin into my nape and lay beside me in the snow and we looked into the sky at the birds rising on the wind. Searching.

He put his hand into my furs and I felt his warm hand on my breast and I felt my chest rising and falling. He put his hot breath into my mouth and I kissed him there on the mountain in the snow and a drop of warm sweat fell down. Oh! I said. He put his warm breath to my mouth and he kissed me and kneaded my flesh and my furs and it made my body come alive, it made me come alive, it made me come alive.

Joe kissed me. Joe made me alive.

FRANKIE, *enthralled, reaches out her good hand to* T-BELLE *and touches her face.*

(*Fiercely.*) He was *mine*. He was my own only thing and now he has seen inside of me. The meanness. The hate I feel for you. He saw it and he will never come back.

FRANKIE *turns away, and as she does so the light goes from her eyes and she switches off as she did earlier.*

'Little jolts', huh? Maybe little bits and pieces burning out of you. That's what I think. Is there a little bit less of you now, Frankie? Just a little? (*Hisses in* FRANKIE's *ear.*) Fizzzzzzz.

FRANKIE *shudders back to life.*

Scene Two

The lights change and the little creepy Chinese tune from the music box recurs. We have entered a liminal space.

FRANKIE *is isolated by the light, and she speaks, at first almost inaudible.*

FRANKIE. Oh, don't *cough*! You're too pale, it's not attractive. '*My English is not fine.*' I'll never leave you, May. I wouldn't do that. Make me an elephant out of lace, May. Make me a giant lace BALLOON and I'll dance inside it! Goddamn! Goddamn! GODDAMN! Oh yes, there's a word!

She lurches forward suddenly to standing.

Good Jesus, this TUB!

The sound of ocean swells and with it we hear the creak and roll of a ship. Lights blaze from the front on FRANKIE, *whose demeanour is now that of* FRANKIE *at seventeen. She speaks very fast, very precise.*

Cold wind flattening my face. Lace at my throat letting in the chill. Hard, honest-to-God ambition swelling me up. What's wrong with that? Taut body under my clothes. Taut, young body under my clothes. My beautiful cream coat edged with sable-coloured velvet. See me! See me! Frances Harmon! Actress! Actress that will be!

A flare of light, a hand to the eye.

Flare of light from the harbour! *Flash!* Here she is! (*American accent.*) Frankie! The Divine Frankie! Frankie La Divine! I'm brightened and – Ah! – displayed! Ah, limelight! Bad for the skin. What are we going to do about that, Frankie? What are we going to do about the lime-corrosive limelight on our springy skin? Weather it! Weather it! Cake on the greasepaint. Cake it on! Make my cheekbones sing a song of razors!

'Come to America with me, my beautiful Irish girl, and there you will yield to me and I will make you my bride! My little bridie and the greatest actress this generation has known. They will know our names the globe across: Junius Brutus Booth Junior and Frances... em Frances...'

Harmon, darling. HARMON.

'Harmon! Oh yes, yes! Of course, my lovely! But soon your
name shall be BOOTH!'

Junius. Fat old fool. Long leather boots. Oh, the thighs! Like
sausages bursting out of their bladders. The sweat-streaked
face under the wig askew, panting over me backstage at the
Aldwych Theatre, London Town. Labouring in his Macheath
gear! Like a pig in a peruke. Labouring over my hot young
body. Trying to sneak inside me. Ha! Like I want your nasty
comical name Junius Brutus Booth *Junior*! I'll have your
connections, thank you, Mr Middling Famous Actor Man in
America. I'll have your tastiest, spiciest *friends* and in return
you shall have whatever you *goddamned* – isn't that what
they say? – whatever you *goddamned* want!

When I land. When I land. When I set my foot on the shores
of America. When this rotten ship gets out of this godforsaken
port of Liverpool and I step away from the filth and stench of
these Irish *spectres*, these pox-ridden poor starving creatures,
then we shall see what other name Frances Harmon requires.
La Divine. The coming woman. Mademoiselle O'Diva.

And now for sustenance.

(*As a vaudevillian.*) With my third last coin I purchased.
From Sedway's Food and Wine Emporium I purchased a
fluffy succulent pillow of buttery rich flaky pastry and their
cheapest bottle of brandy.

Through this next, MAY *comes to stand just behind*
FRANKIE. *As* FRANKIE *describes the pastry, rubbing her
tummy and licking her lips greedily,* MAY *obsessively
focuses on it. She is starving.*

Buttery pastry filled with a rich and oily meaty savoury
filling. Oh, magnificent deliciousness! I shall set it atop my
wonderful *cream-leather valises*!

Watched by MAY, *she does so and elaborately turns her
back on the pastry, winking at the audience.*

And take one last look at the *stews* of Liverpool, before I
fortify myself for my journey to fame and wealth and lovers

without number or wrinkles. Ah! Liverpool! Poor shivering wretched Liverpool!

She stretches out her arms to embrace Liverpool, whilst MAY *grabs the invisible pastry and stuffs it in her mouth without swallowing – using her mouth as a hiding place. Cheeks now distended like a frog's. Stock-still, eyeing* FRANKIE *side-on.* FRANKIE *looks to the pastry. Exaggerated double take that finishes on the pastry. Beat.* MAY *swallows the pastry down in one, the noise of this draws* FRANKIE *around. They stare at each other. Long beat. (Grannie's Footsteps vibe.)* MAY *vomits the pastry extravagantly over* FRANKIE*'s front, and in a second small retch over her 'cream valises'.*

AAAAAAH! My COAT!! You dirty little BITCH! You ratty little piece of filth! Look! Look at what this *repulsive* – this pox-ridden, starving wretch has done to my CREAM COAT!!

She tries to get the attention of the other passengers.

Hello? Excuse me, could you? HELLO! Did anyone see that? I've just been *violated* by this disgusting child! *WILL SOMEONE PAY ATTENTION TO ME????*

She stops dead, seeing the people around her.

Oh my God you're ALL DISGUSTING!

FRANKIE *lets out a panicked and lengthy scream.*

KEEP OFF ME! I'M AN ACTRESS!!!

She pulls MAY *in front of her and, using her as a human shield, backs away from the 'terrifying' crowd.*

Then, a lighting change to a tiny interior space and soundtrack of the interior of a ship – creaking timbers and rain and ocean muffled – indicate that she has taken MAY *to her tiny stateroom.* MAY *lying,* FRANKIE *pacing a tiny defined distance.*

Bitch.

Are you breathing?

Are you BREATHING?

MAY breathes raggedly. FRANKIE pours water on the back of her coat and rubs furiously.

OH! All the perfumes of Arabia will not sweeten this little coat. BLAST YOU! –

MAY dry-retches.

Oh God.

MAY dry-retches.

Oh good Christ!

The ship lurches and both women are thrown once from side to side à la Star Trek.

Good Jesus! This goddamned TUB!

Observes MAY *now.*

YOU'RE TOO THIN! YOU'RE TOO PALE! It's not attractive. It's VILE. And if you die in here I will… Don't you think about starving to death in this stateroom. Do you hear me?

MAY is mesmerised as if by a snake.

I suppose you want cheering up? Hmm?

Right-o.

She sings and does a little, completely inappropriate, sexy 'routine'.

   'Oh Polly you might have toyed and kissed.
   By keeping men off you keep them on.
   But he so pleased me and he so teased me.
   What I did you must have done.'

MAY is staring at her, terrified.

Oh, get up!

I suppose you're hungry. Or thirsty. I suppose we can organise some milk for you. (*As if to a deaf person.*) *MILK? FOR YOU?*

MAY practically jumps up the cabin wall and remains pinned halfway up the wall.

Oh, for the love of God. Just *calm down*! *Relaxez vous!*
French. You're just a baby really, aren't you? I shall tell you
a story. Once upon a time there was a beautiful actress
named Frances. Here, have a sup of brandy... Don't
CHOKE! Now, Frances was the belle of PHIBS BUH RUH.
In Dublin. Where the hell are you from? (*To amuse herself*.)
THE ORIENT! Oh, interesting. Good. Well, Phibsborough is
almost exactly like the Orient only a little different. More
pigs. HA HA HA!

MAY *looks baffled throughout*.

Nobody in Phibsborough knew what a marvellous creature
Frances was but one day she left! Sailed across the bitter
seas and came to London! I imagine you haven't been?

Looks for an answer. Bored now.

Anyway. Back to me.

MAY. Srnmmm.

FRANKIE. Jesus God!

MAY (*with an effort*). *Maith agat*.

FRANKIE. Come again?

MAY. Thank you.

FRANKIE. Oh. Don't mention it. I was talking.

MAY. Sorry.

FRANKIE. Don't mention it. Milk?

MAY. Milk. Yes. Milk.

FRANKIE. Oh God. I'm nearly down to my last... No! It's
fine! Have some milk!

MAY. Thank you.

FRANKIE. How's the Orient this weather anyway?

MAY (*slowly and deliberately*). I don't understand.

FRANKIE. Oh God! It was a – Have you been listening?

MAY. Em...

FRANKIE. WHY DO PEOPLE NEVER LISTEN!

MAY. Sorry. I don't…

FRANKIE. Yes?

MAY. My English is not fine.

FRANKIE. Oh. You're one of those Fenians, I suppose… Well,
LISTEN. Just try harder! Now, where was I?

*Sudden lighting and soundtrack change. The two women
stand facing front.*

MAY *carrying* FRANKIE*'s valises, light blinding them from
the front, soundtrack of New York street: horses clopping,
people shouting and church bells clanging.* MAY *nervous,*
FRANKIE *exultant.*

Booth's Olympic Theatre, New York City! Look at it, May.
(*Reading.*) Now Playing: *Riddle Me Rita* starring Ada
Breckenbauer and Junius Brutus Booth Junior. *Ça Commence!*

MAY. I'm sorry, Frances?

Beat.

FRANKIE (*to the ether*). Call me Frankie.

Scene Three

The next day. Morning light.

MAY *is tending to* FRANKIE, *who is noticeably more alert.*
MAY *plays with her as you would with a child, tipping her nose
with a flannel.*

MAY. Oh Polly, you might have toyed and kissed. (*Bang on the
nose with the flannel.*)

FRANKIE *laughs.*

By keeping men off you keep them on! (*Double bang on the
nose.*)

FRANKIE *laughs more.*

FRANKIE *seems to get it. Laughing in an uninhibited manner – that is quite disturbing.* MAY *is delighted. She is 'in there'.*

Oh yes, beautiful girl! You're right in there, aren't you? We'll have to watch ourselves, won't we? We'll have to be careful what we say around you now!

MAY *doesn't yet grasp that* FRANKIE *is responding to the flannel gesture and not the words, which she can't understand. Throughout,* FRANKIE *responds to the tone of voice and the facial expressions of those who talk to her. She can't process the words.*

(*Smiling.*) And T-Belle's gone to fetch the doctor to make you better.

FRANKIE *smiles back.*

Aha! You DO understand. Good girl!

(*Takes* FRANKIE*'s face in her two hands. Seriously.*) You need to watch what you do now. She'll write you off like – (*Click of fingers.*) THAT! She will.

FRANKIE *laughs delightedly at the finger-click.*

NO! No. You need to be serious, Frankie. You need to take this seriously.

FRANKIE, *responding to* MAY*'s serious face, is de-mirthed.*

Exactly. Put a real 'face' on you if she starts talking about leaving or you being 'gone' or any of that old guff. I'm serious now, Frankie. She's gone very peculiar since she's been off on her own up there, you wouldn't know where she was got, so don't let her any little bit of quarter now. Do you mind me? It's back to you and me now, *a chroí*. Just us Injuns, isn't that it?

Beat. FRANKIE *has a serious face on her now.* FRANKIE *concentrates very hard on frowning at* MAY.

I'm going to ask you something now, Frankie, and I want you to be very honest with me. Now, don't spare me. I want to know.

MAY gathers herself by lowering her head. FRANKIE follows her gesture to the floor, trying to see what it is that MAY is looking for.

What are you at? Pay attention! Now. Frankie. Now, my dear.

Beat.

Why won't you talk to me?

FRANKIE, skewered by MAY's gaze, tries to vocalise in a puzzled manner.

FRANKIE. Wuh wuh wuh, wooh wooh wuh wuh!!!

This continues over the beginning of the next paragraph as far as 'It's not all about me.'

MAY. No! No! I hear what you're saying. You've a lot on your mind and it's not all about me. Those are all good points. But nonetheless. It's something I have to say to you.

Well. I'll be frank. Frankie. It's *hurtful* I don't mind admitting. It's *painful* to me. And there I've said it out. And I'd like it to stop if you don't mind. And if there's something on your mind – even an *old* something, I'd rather you told me than let this – dogged silence lie between us. Now there I've said it.

Beat.

It's just that sometimes, since… You know. I feel like you're looking right inside my head. Winkling out every little mean thought I have in there like you was shucking oysters.

FRANKIE laughs at MAY's 'winkling-out' mime.

Yes, I know it's batty but that's what it feels like anyhow. But, Frankie. If you can see… inside me, and if there's one big thing that's making you… huff so. Well. I don't think I could bear that. So take a deep breath, Frankie dear, and get it off your chest once and for all.

MAY takes in her hands FRANKIE's good one and, gently, the bad one, and takes a deep breath 'with' FRANKIE.

Now. Why won't you talk to me?

T-BELLE enters.

(*Urgent whisper, dropping* FRANKIE*'s hands and
exaggeratedly acting 'normal'*.) Right. Remember what I
said. Be very cool with her. Not a word for a cat. We'll keep
our hour. Ssh!

T-BELLE *empties a bundle on the table. It contains a modest
amount of food. Flatbread, a couple of tins and some hard
cheese.*

T-BELLE. I suppose you won't be needing this. I imagine
young Mr Ferren dropped off a goose while I was out.

MAY. There's no need to be like that.

T-BELLE *busies herself with the food.*

Where did you – [*get the food.*]

T-BELLE. Don't bother asking me.

Beat.

Can she eat? That, I mean. Can she eat regular food.

MAY (*including* FRANKIE, *as always*). What a question!

T-BELLE. Dr Fenniman said she mightn't be able to swallow
properly any more. That she might choke. He said he told
you that. Does she choke?

MAY. She's an excellent trencher woman.

T-BELLE. Appetite of a bird you said.

MAY. She *doesn't choke.*

T-BELLE. Alright, Mamma.

MAY (*going to the food to prepare it*). Leave that to me.

T-BELLE. She smells clean.

MAY. She is clean.

Beat.

And before you start on, you don't have to have anything to
do with keeping her clean. She wouldn't want you to – She
doesn't want anyone else to help her out while she's...

poorly. You can put that right out of your mind. If you're worried about all that.

T-BELLE. Fine.

MAY. You talked to the doctor.

T-BELLE. I did. He told me exactly what he told you, Mamma. Exactly.

MAY. I see. Good.

T-BELLE. Oh, Mamma.

MAY. Hsst! (*Indicating* FRANKIE, *who is looking alert and curious.*)

T-BELLE. He told me how it would be –

MAY. Did he mention what the cousin said about her?

T-BELLE. He said that there'd be more… jolts. That she's… (*Lowers her voice in response to* MAY*'s evident distress at* FRANKIE *'overhearing'.*) that she might be shutting down, Mamma. Bit by bit –

MAY. Did he tell you what the wife's cousin said about her in *The Winter's Tale*? Did he?

She goes behind FRANKIE *and strokes her head, and* T-BELLE *can see that* MAY *is upset.*

T-BELLE. Well… Yes, Mamma. He did.

MAY. And what did he say?? What, T-Belle?

T-BELLE. He said. He said.

MAY. Don't look at me! Look at her! She's right here!

Beat.

She's terribly lonely, T-Belle! Talk to her! *Please!*

T-BELLE (*turning to* FRANKIE. *Unconvincingly at first – she is not used to lying*). He said he never saw anything so… majestic. So… moving.

FRANKIE *looks blank so* T-BELLE *tries the words with mime.*

Majestic. (*Inappropriate mime*.) Moving. (*Inappropriate mime*.)

FRANKIE *turns a puzzled face to* MAY.

MAY. Which bit?

T-BELLE. What?

MAY. Which bit did he say was majestic and moving, T-Belle.

T-BELLE. The bit. The bit where she had no lines. The bit where the other one says… 'Music. Awake her. Strike… Let' all that… I can't remember, Mamma. I usen't to listen.

MAY. 'Music! Awake her! Strike! Be stone no more!'

Show what she used to do, T-Belle! When she'd jump up from the chair and come to all slow and turney.

T-BELLE (*deeply uncomfortable*). I wouldn't be able to –

MAY. Show her what we're talking about! Come on, Tee!

'Music! Awake her! Strike!'

T-BELLE *strikes the statue pose reluctantly.* FRANKIE *is interested. Good hand on chin, pensive, comically so.*

Then something something something… Oh Lord, my memory…

'Strike all who look upon with marble!'

T-BELLE (*pedantically from her statue pose*). Marvel.

MAY. Marvel.

T-BELLE, *stiffly and hammily, begins to 'come to life'. A bit more Frankenstein's monster than queen.* FRANKIE *begins to laugh, delighted.* T-BELLE *taking it all very seriously,* MAY *delighted by* FRANKIE's *delight and finishes the speech in triumph.*

'Be stone no more,
Bequeath to death thy numbness, for from him
Dear life redeems you. – You perceive she stirs!'

At this she breaks off, and T-BELLE *and* MAY *stare at* FRANKIE *as she continues to laugh and laugh.*

(*Recovering*.) Well, that was a tonic! A tonic for her.

T-BELLE. Mamma, she doesn't under–

MAY. Oh, you think you know everything. Well! That is the best yet. I haven't seen that spark for a long month.

There is a loud knocking at the door. MAY *and* T-BELLE *freeze.* FRANKIE*'s laughter continues.*

T-BELLE. Take her inside, Mamma. I'm expecting someone.

MAY. Who?

T-BELLE. I'll explain later, Mamma, just –

The door swings open and NELLY THE PIG *enters. Sumptuously dressed in a weird assortment of furs and lace. Young, supremely confident and hard.*

NELLY. Well, wayhay! It's a party!

T-BELLE. Nelly.

MAY (*to* T-BELLE, *not quite sotto*). Nelly the Pig?

NELLY. Oh well, that is just lovely! (*Turns to go.*)

T-BELLE. No, Nelly! I'm sorry about my mother. She and Frankie are just going to… (*Pointedly to* MAY.) retire.

NELLY. Well, they're both about the right age. Ba-boom!

Ooh! Frankie. Look at *you*!

MAY *takes* FRANKIE *in the bath chair to the side room,* FRANKIE *looking over her shoulder at* NELLY, *vocalising, upset at being taken away from the 'party'.*

Beat.

Well, that's some sight! What *is* that? Did her brain… What, fall out?

T-BELLE. Something like that. Thanks for coming.

NELLY. Oh, I wouldn't have missed this for… diamonds!

T-BELLE. You're not here to gawk.

NELLY. *Au contraire!* French. I'm here precisely to gawk. You've suddenly become the most entertaining *shack* in the city of Skag. Well... *Environs*.

Jeez. So Frankie's an imbecile. Who'da thunk it. You got liquor?

T-BELLE. No.

NELLY. Oh. (*Making to go.*) WHAT a gip.

T-BELLE (*going to her pack and extracting a bottle of clear liquid*). Here.

NELLY. Ah. Trail gut-rot. Excellent. Hiding it from the booze hound? Or doesn't she drink now? (*Taking an extravagant swig from the bottle.*) Ooh! Yes. I think I might just *pig* this whole thing down in one. What do you think, Mrs ManWoman? You guys are Irish, right? You should be used to having a *pig* in the parlour. Oink oink.

T-BELLE. That's just a name some people –

NELLY. Oh, I know why I have *that* name. And believe me, if you knew you would take it as a compliment as I do. *Oink oink! MMMMMmmm!* I just don't like hearing it from lemony mouths like your little Irish mammy.

T-BELLE. My mother has been under a lot of –

NELLY. But perhaps you have a little inkling of piggery yourself these days from what I've heard. A little *oinkling...* What are you doing down here in smellsville, T-Belle? Didn't work out with your little *Injun*?

T-BELLE, *furious, indicates to the side room, urging* NELLY *to lower her voice.* NELLY *shifts to a theatrical stage whisper, taunting* T-BELLE *by occasionally 'forgetting' to lower her voice and having to 'shushh!' herself.*

Joe, wasn't it? Or maybe that's just his white name. Jumba Linga Wimbo Joe-ba? Something like that? News does travel! He's built I'll tell you. We were all most impressed up at the Nugget at mysterious little Weirdname T-Belle bagging such a *prize!* Ooh! SSSSH! *Silly me!* Well, no harm done! We figured he was hitched for good, but it all worked out for everyone, didn't it? I'm sure it won't be long before he's snuffling back down here again to us now that he's lost his little whitey wifey to the dummy in there.

She sees T-BELLE *is close to tears.*

Oops! Have I said something I shouldn't? Oi!

T-BELLE (*recovering*).You're a regular telegraph office, you know that, Nelly.

NELLY *takes this in. Beat.*

NELLY. Funny thing that. The telegraph office. Your Frankie was in there often enough playing poker with the poor saps who came in there: *desperate* to send word back to the little wife at home in smallstown. Always had to wait to send a message, funnily enough. And there was always a coincidental game of poker going on in the back parlour of that office. Again. Funnily enough.

As she talks, she pokes about the house, idly and rudely opening jars and looking behind hung clothes. While she instinctively cases the joint, she swigs from the bottle.

I played them myself, naturally. Took so long to send a telegraph home that they always lost just a little too much money. Just a touch. Not enough to stop 'em coming back, of course. Trudging back through the mud to send another reassuring message home to the frau and kinderlings.

And then there was that long lonely night to fill, what with the rekindled memories of home and no word *ever* coming back for some reason, and a touch too much liquor swilled down over the cards – always a chance of a lonely man needing a bit of comfort – well! The fragrant Frankie in there – (*A gesture to indicate the side room.*) will bear me out here. Always money to be made in the *telegraph office*. But you know the funniest thing of all, T-Belle? Huh?

T-BELLE. No.

NELLY (*takes another extravagant slug of the trail gut-rot*). *No wires.* Not one. Well, not one that went anywhere. Not one telegram into or out of that shack in two years. It was all smoke and mirrors. And poker. And – how can I put this –

Well, let's just say me and your auntie doing what we do best. Did best. (*Music-hall flourish*.) Thaaaaaa-t's Skagway!

Beat.

T-BELLE. You proud of taking money from poor saps trying to make their fortune?

NELLY. Oh now, don't try to be stupider than you look… Those hordes of men down there wandering round like spectres? 'Tain't gold fever they have. Just want adventure and to be some place else. By the time they stagger over the pass to Skagway it's all run out of them like little flat balloons. The most they're fit for is to spend whatever they've got left on a bit of tail or a bottle of forgetting. They're not the real thing like you, little Injun T-Belle.

What kind of a name is that anyway?

T-BELLE *is silent.*

Oh, you can tell your Auntie Nelly. Humour me. Indulge me. Garner my goodwill with a little light-hearted banter. As it were.

Beat.

T-BELLE. My mother wanted to call me Theresa. After her mother.

NELLY. Oh, stop! Don't tell me! And *Frankie* favoured Belle. Oh, delicious! So Frankie got top billing, *Mamma* got reduced to a little Tee, and T-Belle got a name far more exotic than she. Oh, dear. Oh, dearie dear me.

T-BELLE. That's just about it.

NELLY. See how pleasantly go the minutes when a little conversational give-and-take occurs?

She slugs down the last of the liquor, turns over the bottle and lets it roll to the floor.

Alrighty. You have bored me to death and run out of booze. So before you have the pleasure of watching my lily-white ass sashaying out the door, are you going to tell me what you want?

T-BELLE. A dance.

NELLY. Well, if I've heard that once I've heard it a million times! But I imagine you're not going to go sweaty gropey on me. Or are you? You're a queer type, T-Belle… (*A sudden thought.*) T-Belle what?

T-BELLE. Sorry?

NELLY. T-Belle?… (*Clicking her fingers in* T-BELLE*'s face like an impatient teacher.*) What? Who's your daddy?

Beat.

T-BELLE. He was a soldier. He died in the war.

NELLY. Oh! How tragic.

T-BELLE. He was.

NELLY. Of course he was. Neat.

Beat.

You know Soapy – have mercy on him – used to swear that Frankie was a puffy soft *man* –

T-BELLE. Stoppit.

NELLY. Maybe that's why he investigated.

T-BELLE. *Stoppit!*

NELLY. Do beg. (*Beat. Reading something in* T-BELLE*'s face.*) 'Pologies. Overstepped the whatchacallit. Mark.

Beat.

Well, I'll go first, shall I? We've all been *breathless* in anticipation of what might – *occur* – within the lace *structure* that has been being – *erected* – saving your presence – in the New Criterion. It's a bit patchy. But impressive I will say. Liberty. Statue of. Lit from within. Bit of a *tease*. Makes you wonder what the hell the old trout was going to *do* in there. Well, hell, *I'm* curious.

T-BELLE. When the statue was unveiled. Frankie was famous.

NELLY. Oh, I know! Word is! Yes.

T-BELLE. Well, famous for one role. She danced inside a lace replica of Liberty doing her most famous scene. Hermione in *A Winter's Tale*. Shakespeare.

NELLY. Never heard of that one.

T-BELLE. Well, it's a lesser-known –

NELLY. I didn't say I cared!

T-BELLE. She played a statue coming to life. Cried her white make-up off every night. Her party trick. She could turn on real tears just like – (*Snaps fingers.*) that! It impressed the audience because they couldn't do it. Sleight of hand. Made them think she could act. So when she danced it was a real nine-day wonder. It was prettily done too. Tastefully lit. Very few clothes. It was a sensation, in the day.

NELLY. A sensation! Lord.

T-BELLE. They made souvenirs.

NELLY. Do you say? So dear old Frankie spun out her party trick. Good for her!

T-BELLE (*irritated*). Look.

T-BELLE *goes to the box of lace and bobbins and takes out the music box of the Statue of Liberty.*

(*Reading from the base of the music box.*) 'A Celebration of Liberty, Souvenir and Music Box, E. Mason, New York, 1886.'

She *winds it up and lets the weird little tune play and the statue turns round and round.* NELLY, *despite herself, is mesmerised. The two women look at the music box until the tune slowly turns discordant with slowness.*

NELLY. Yowzah!

T-BELLE. I need you to take her place. Tomorrow night. You don't have to do anything much. Just take your clothes off and sway.

NELLY. I can do that any time.

T-BELLE. Not like this. I'll pay you two and a half thou. And anything that gets thrown up on the stage. You won't make that on your back. Skagway is over.

NELLY. Well, a fool could tell you that.

Beat.

Now why would you pay me all that money for one show in a rebuilt clapboard music hall halfway up a mountain.

T-BELLE. Because it's a con.

NELLY. You have my undivided attention.

T-BELLE. My dribbling fool of an aunt signed a paper that locked all my gold into the New Criterion. And I need you to dance it out of there. Frankie signed a paper with Jed and Soapy. Five thousand for a dance and he's sticking to it. But 'The famous Liberty Dance of Frances J. Harmon' is what it says. 'Of'. Not 'by'.

NELLY. Sneaky. A cool two and a half?

T-BELLE. And anything that gets thrown up to the stage you can keep.

NELLY. Generous. (*Raises the empty liquor bottle ruefully.*) Liberty!

T-BELLE. Will you do it?

NELLY. And tell me, T-Belle No-name. What makes you think Jed will give you the money even if there is a dance? I mean, have you *met* him?

T-BELLE. He will. He will because… Because if he doesn't… (*Looks around theatrically, 'Can I trust you?'*)

T-BELLE *moves closer to* NELLY *until she has her back against a wall.*

NELLY. Ya-hah?

T-BELLE. If he doesn't…

T-BELLE *takes a knife from a leather gunpowder pouch. It is made of gold. The handle an elaborately worked eagle. She holds it towards* NELLY.

I'll cut his throat.

NELLY. Jeezum H.

T-BELLE. Or yours, if you cross me.

NELLY. Alright, Tiger Lady! I gotcha. Easy now.

T-BELLE *does not alter her position.*

Yeah! Yeah! You're a real bona fida *threat*. What kin I tell you? I take you real serious. I am... trans*formed* in my appreciation of you. Genuine player. Full of surprises. Just put the pretty slicer away, willya??

T-BELLE *ignores her, although the threat is not really to* NELLY. NELLY *is wary as hell now, however.*

T-BELLE. I just don't care any more, Nelly. Way I feel about now I could just go over to his lush little room up there in the *new* Criterion right this minute and slash him open with this little beauty, sharpen it back up nice on his scrawny neck bone and empty his coffers.

NELLY. Like I said I gotcha. Have your point there, Tee, I'm with you, buddy.

T-BELLE. See? The thing inside me that'd stop me? The thing that made me feel like I didn't want to be a *bad* girl, made me 'fraid of being *damned*? 'Sgone. Things like that don't matter up here, you know? The sky's too big or something. I don't know what it is, Nelly the Pig. Anyhows. That thing that'd stop me slitting a throat, well it's finally flown out the window all of a sudden just like her brain. (*Jerk of thumb to* FRANKIE.) That answer your question?

NELLY. Comprehensively.

T-BELLE *lowers the knife.*

So what's stopping you goin' over there right now? Reclaiming your stash.

T-BELLE. Getting caught. Don't wanna get strung up like the poor sap who done Soapy. So we make it legal. Ish. Right about now we're all square. So you dance for Jed and get me my money and you get half.

NELLY. And if he doesn't play ball? I get nothing.

T-BELLE. If he doesn't play ball... Right after I use it on him
I'll give you this.

NELLY *goes to touch the knife.* T-BELLE *recoils, but holds
it so* NELLY *can see it.*

NELLY. Pretty. That's Injun work. Right?

T-BELLE. Yup.

NELLY. Sentimental value I bet.

T-BELLE. Oh yeah.

NELLY. Gold wouldn't make much of a knife though. A fool
could tell you that. It's plated, right? There's not more than
fifty dollars' worth of gold in that. Tops.

T-BELLE. The knife's plated.

NELLY. Figures.

T-BELLE. But the handle. The handle is one piece.

NELLY. *One piece? Solid? Crapola!*

T-BELLE. It came out of the Yukon River in '78. Before a
single white man had crossed the Chilkoot Pass.

NELLY. I never heard of a nugget that big.

T-BELLE. You wouldn't have. *Whitey.*

NELLY. Well, there's no need to be unpleasant. And how'd you
get it?

T-BELLE (*with some difficulty*). A parting gift.

NELLY. Ooh! He must have wanted rid of you bad...

T-BELLE *grips the knife with intent.*

(*Remembering who she is dealing with.*) A thousand
apologies. I misspoke.

Beat.

Well. Now that we've shared so much I could scarcely
refuse. But T-Belle? A word to the wise. And now, don't take

this the wrong way cos you're kinda on a hair-trigger there if you'll forgive me saying so...

T-BELLE (*re-sheathes the knife and turns away*). I'm listening.

NELLY *grabs* T-BELLE *by the hair and turns her to face her.*

NELLY. If you cross me I'll cut *your* throat.

NELLY *releases* T-BELLE *and flounces out the door. Long beat.* MAY *enters with* FRANKIE.

MAY. I heard the door.

T-BELLE *is silent.*

I'll put this outside. (*A bundle of clothes –* T-BELLE *recoils from the smell.*)

You don't have to do anything with it. (*Leaves.*)

T-BELLE *goes to replace the music box in the trunk. Then she has a thought. She releases a mechanism underneath the box and opens a secret compartment. She puts the gold knife carefully inside it and replaces the music box.* FRANKIE *watches her.*

T-BELLE *is uncomfortable being left with* FRANKIE. *She moves about the room, 'fixing' things and looking back once or twice, sees* FRANKIE *following her with her eyes, curiously.*

T-BELLE. Stop looking at me.

She attempts to 'be alone'. But FRANKIE's *gaze disconcerts her. Tries to ignore her. Can't.* T-BELLE *hunkers down and talks to* FRANKIE *real close. Conscious always of the door and that* MAY *might come in at any moment.*

She's right. You *are* in there. Oh, I can see you, Frankie. See you in there watching. Are you thrilled with yourself? Are you delighted you've found a way to have your *entourage* back? The whole little coterie back dancing attendance on you. You old slut!

'We have to go to Cleveland. Your Auntie Frankie has a big job, it'll be just what we've waited for. Now don't you put that face on you, Tee, it's progress and that's all there is about it.'

And there we'd be. Stuck in some terrible digs, letting out your costumes and painting your name bigger on the playbills in the night: *hated* by everyone. Running out in the middle of the night with our stuff piled onto a cart because you messed it up *again*. You baby. You mean needy drunk.

James Ferren found me. He came over to me as I was sitting like a child in the snow, waking up to the day of glorious work and he told me.

'You have to come back. Your Auntie Frankie has had a stroke.'

Something rushed up inside me: a raging billious thing and I spread out my two hands and dived down into the snow and I screamed with all the power in my lungs. I raged for all the rottenness and stagnation that had come through the night to grasp me.

I waited for Joe to fall on me and hold me to him and power his good flesh against mine and make it go away. I looked up with the dregs of my howling falling from my mouth and I could see it all in his eyes. This woman is not whole. This woman who I loved is not a right woman. I knew he would not come down the mountain with me to the cabin where you waited for me and May waited for me. Smelling of sick and shit.

FRANKIE *remains stock-still as* T-BELLE *rises to leave.*

Let's see where that mother of mine has got to. Don't fall over, I'll be back in a moment.

A thought makes her turn back.

Or do.

She leaves and FRANKIE *is alone.*

Scene Four

FRANKIE *jolts back into awareness. She is troubled. Seeing the same image again and again.*

MAY *is there. Young. A mantle of lace over her hair. Lit by a harsh single light. Her back to us. She raises her hand as to the frame of a door and turns slowly, fragile, before 'going through' the door.*

FRANKIE. Don't look at me. Don't look at me, May.

A loud fizzing sound and a quick blackout. When the single light springs up again, harsh, FRANKIE *is no longer lit. Just* MAY. *She repeats the action, but this time her face is a mask.*

Just keep walking, May, don't turn around. It's such a little thing I'm asking. It's nothing. Don't look at me. Just walk through the door and do the little thing I'm asking you. The tiny little thing I'm asking you.

MAY *turns again and walks through the door.* FRANKIE *walks to the 'door frame' with her back to it and speaks to someone. Procuring. Sotto voce.*

Pure. Such purity. *I* won't do, I understand that. You want something special. Something... different.

I've seen you looking, you know. Oh, I've seen the way you look at her. I know you have a taste for the simple. I watched you yesterday. Watching her sewing. The needle slipping under my skirts like a tiny flash of lightning. Her fingers slipping under the hem. Precise. Delicate. Concentrating so fiercely on her task she doesn't even see you. It's... a tease, no? Builds up inside you I should expect. Like an urge.

To possess the mundane, the normal. Sully it a little – it's entirely understandable. Especially a man in your position *immersed* as you are in the world of theatricality, one can tire of the exotic. One's palate gets a bit jaded. I can help you there.

The loud fizzing sound accompanies a sudden blackout. Then MAY *is harshly, singly lit again. She turns again. Her expression is blank. The fizzing sound remains under* FRANKIE's *words.*

You know what I want, don't you? You're quite clear of what is required?

MAY *turns back again in a sudden harsh light, blank as before.*

Hermione. '*Music! Awake her! Strike!*' You won't be disappointed. By her or me.

MAY *turns again, as before.*

Oh, it's a done deal. She owes me. Happy to do it. She'll do anything for me. You see… I saved her life. Long ago. Yes. We go back a long way, May and I.

MAY *turns again, as before.*

May. Yes. You may. (*A laugh.*)

But you musn't take this lightly. Innocence is given only once. So have her. And cherish it in your memory for ever.

MAY *turns for the last time. Lights cut. Fizzing sound rises along with discordant held notes of strings. In* MAY*'s place is* T-BELLE, *wearing the same lace around her head. Affecting the ecstatic expression of St Theresa of Avila.*

(*With contempt.*) Innocence.

The fizzing sound cuts out and the lights 'normalise'. T-BELLE *takes a book from under her arm and sets it on the floor. She tries again to imitate the picture in the book,* Great Works of Art. *After a moment:*

And what, little woman, are you meant to be?

T-BELLE. St Theresa of Avila.

FRANKIE. Show me that. (*Looks at the illustration.*) And what is St Theresa of Avila doing, might I ask?

T-BELLE. Praying to God.

FRANKIE *drops the book and grabs* T-BELLE*'s face. Fierce.*

FRANKIE. And what, dearest T-Belle, is St Theresa of Avila *thinking*?

T-BELLE. She looks kind of sick in her stomach, but she don't seem to mind. I think that angel with the arrow is gonna kill her.

FRANKIE. Oh, he's killing her alright. You know, T-Belle, I know what Theresa of Avila is thinking. Would you like to know what that is?

T-BELLE. No.

FRANKIE. Well, I'm going to tell you anyway. Once upon a time, when your mother and I first came to New York, I spent some time... working. Well, not as I do now – as an actress, but around the – ahem – fringes of the theatrical milieu.

T-BELLE. Huh?

FRANKIE. Same sort of thing. Night work. Anyway! While I was – learning my craft, I met a very wise woman from a place called France and she told me some secrets that she had learned. Some very secret, very delicious words.

T-BELLE. I don't want to know any secrets.

FRANKIE. Well, don't worry, *ma petite*, you won't understand them. Yet! But you must listen very carefully, because one day you will and it will safeguard you from a whole lot of damned nonsense you're gonna hear.

T-BELLE. That's swearing.

FRANKIE. *Nonetheless!* St Theresa, in my humble opinion, is suffering from *la petite mort*, the little death. She is feeling *hochite Wallung*, she feels the fury of love, *la praline en délire...*

T-BELLE (*hides under the lace*). I'm finished talking about St There–

FRANKIE. She is wandering in the dark garden, the hill of sedge, the children's palace, the red chamber –

T-BELLE. Stoppit! –

FRANKIE. She is rejoicing in her innermost knot, her precious crucible, her pillow of musk, her fragrant grass...

T-BELLE. Stoppit, Auntie Frankie!

FRANKIE. Above all, child, she is *not* praying to that big bearded God your mamma makes so much of. Because Theresa is all that Theresa will ever need. And you must never ever trust anyone who tells you how to be or what to do or who to love. You must never trust anyone, T-Belle. (*Holds* T-BELLE's *face again.*) *Not ever.* Because people are filthy, self-serving dogs.

She releases T-BELLE. *Beat.*

T-BELLE. What happened to the lady from France?

FRANKIE. She died.

T-BELLE. Is she in Heaven?

FRANKIE. No one, *no one* is in Heaven.

Lights on the pair to black. The fizzing noise louder and louder through the following. FRANKIE *is not seen, only her voice is heard over a repeated harsh spotlight that comes and goes on* MAY, *turning to* FRANKIE *from the doorway, blank.*

Just keep walking, May, don't turn around. It's just a little thing I'm asking you. It's nothing, it's as nothing. Trust me. Offer it up. Trust me.

The harsh discordant strings play and the fizzing sound rises to a climax. Lights change to the next scene. FRANKIE *switches on to the present.*

Scene Five

FRANKIE *alone. Afternoon. The door opens slowly.* FRANKIE *does not respond, does not hear it.* NELLY *cautiously enters, an overblown white-feather fan, obviously a music-hall prop, in her hand. She props the door of the cabin open with a largish case. She goes to the side room and checks that there is no one there. Checks the gunpowder pouch and is furious to discover it empty.*

She approaches FRANKIE, *who finally sees her and responds with a childlike and trusting delight.*

NELLY (*smiling all the while and making all the right faces for*
    FRANKIE). Yes! It's me! Hello, dummy! Oh yes, you're
    happy to see me, you poor maniac! Yes! NELLY! Yes! Your
    old sparring partner, you dumb, poor, brain-damaged idiot!!
    Oh my, you sure are a ruined piece of human. Yes you are!
    Yes and… What?

FRANKIE *is pointing excitedly at* NELLY*'s nice coat.*

Yes! I look nice! Yes, uh-huh you betcha! Yes I surely do…
    And you… You look… nice… too! Yes! (*Pointing at*
    FRANKIE *'admiringly'*.) Look at you, dummy! Yes, lovely!

*She 'idly' lifts a few more lids and looks under a few more
things.* FRANKIE *looks eagerly inquisitive.*

Hmmm? Oh, nothing. Just looking around the old
    homestead… Seeing whatcha got! Lots of nice…
    whatchacallit… stuff. Mmmm. All very nice. All. Very. Nice.

FRANKIE *spots the fan. Delight. Pointing.*

Oh yes! This. THIS IS FOR YOU. FOR YOU. (*Pointing to
    the fan and to* FRANKIE.) Yes. For you! A little subterfuge.
    Yes! A *faux entrée*! Yes! Because I love you so much, you
    weird little bit of a woman! Out of the goodness of my heart
    I trudged over from the panic at the docks to give you a tatty
    feathery piece of crap! Yes I did!

Gives it to FRANKIE, *who spends the next while smiling
and oohing and trying to unfurl the fan with her one good
hand.* NELLY *talks now ostensibly to* FRANKIE *but more to
herself, while she tears the cabin apart, searching.*

Now where, Frankie girl, would our dearest Theresa Belle
    hide her *valuables*? Huh? Well, of course I'd love to stay and
    earn it, but quite frankly, *Frankie*, if there's a sensible soul
    left here by sundown tomorrow I'll be more than a little
    surprised. Bit of a change of plan. Turns out old Jed has
    shipped most of that gold out already. Of course, he wasn't
    going to tell poor old T-Belle that! Nope, probably going to
    try the old double-cross on her and risk getting his silly old
    windpipe slit! Yes, the naughty old moo! Trouble is my
    money'd be on that pretty golden eagle ending up in

T-Belle's little gullet... Oh yes indeedy! And old Nelly would be left with *nada*. And Nelly doesn't like the sound of that one little bit, Frankie girl! Now where the hell is the goddamned thing!

So I'm shipping out tonight. Once I reclaim a little something I've set my heart on taking with me. (*Hands on knees, smiling and talking to* FRANKIE *as to a tiny toddler.*) Yes I am! I'm stealing a birdie and then stealing away! You see what I did there?

She gets up and resumes her search. None too worried about the mess she's causing.

It's a little thing called the sourdough grapevine, I'm afraid, Frankie m'dear. A word to the wise from the unscrupulous and before you know it a fine big ship that no one knew about appears on the dock and all the smart people magically appear and sail away on it. Yes! Yes they do! Pity really. I very much doubt your *entourage* up at the Criterion will get wind of it. Too busy fretting with lace and fussing about the limelights. All excited about tonight – The *big event*! *The show!* The *Dummkopfs*!

But you have to be selective, don't you? I mean to say, if they'd let the woodlice stow away on the ark they wouldn't have got very far now, would they? Not that I'm much of a Bible woman myself – Goddamit! (*Flinging some detritus away from her violently.*) Where is the goddamn bird!

FRANKIE, *thoughtfully, having succeeded in opening the fan, bats it coquettishly, then, with the practice of years, suddenly snaps it shut and points it purposefully towards the trunk that* NELLY *has been emptying.* NELLY *is arrested by the unexpectedly purposeful movement and interprets it as a clue.* FRANKIE *mechanically repeats the gesture – rehearsing it.* NELLY *carefully re-searches the trunk, continually checking in with the pointing fan, until she comes to the Statue of Liberty souvenir.* FRANKIE *recognises it and waves the fan at it delightedly.*

Oh, you beauty!

She ravenously opens the music box and takes out the golden eagle knife. FRANKIE is delighted. 'Pretty!' And NELLY pockets it.

Well, you, as my grandmother used to say, are as useful as a small pot!

The music box is playing its strange Chinese tune. It arrests NELLY for a moment.

That's nice. Peaceful. *Bonne chance*, Frankie m'dear.

She goes to the door to leave, but, perhaps recalled by the music, she turns. It should recall, in some way, MAY's turn at the door.

I'm glad you like the fan.

She goes. FRANKIE gently fans herself, the picture of a southern belle, and stares at the music box, as the lights change.

Scene Six

Lights change to strange, then back to normal. With the change of lights comes a soundtrack: the now familiar fizzing sound of FRANKIE's memory and gradually a louder 'white' sound, very like the sound you hear when your ears are under the water in a bath. Ordinary sounds that happen through the scene are heightened or lowered randomly. When MAY and T-BELLE enter later, their voices are incomprehensible, distended and distant, part of the swooping soundtrack. Above or through these noises is the voice of FRANKIE. These words are happening in her head in real time. Now. Her voice is on the soundtrack. She raises her head and looks about.

FRANKIE (*voice-over*). Where's the smiler? Where's the old one with the soft hands and the 'Ah! That's it!' Where's the one with the smiling and the cheese! I want some cheese. (*Pause. Looks about. Nothing has happened.*)

I WANT SOME FUCKING CHEESE! Hello????? Hello?
Smiler???? I want some nice tasty salty-in-the-mouth cheese.
CHEEEEEEESE!!! Stupid everybody. Stupid things.
Nobody here. Helllloooo??? No. All alone. Am I? Am I all
alone? Hmmm. Hope long-face doesn't come back. Nice
here with me and smiler. It was nice. Nice just sitting here
with that one. Doing things I want.

*Leans back as something comes over her. Then the familiar
switching off occurs and she stops stock-still as a little jolt of
memory overtakes her as it burns from her. This memory is
bookended by the fizzing sound. During the following, MAY
and T-BELLE enter, exhausted, they cannot be heard by the
audience, just an increase in the white noise of the
soundtrack. FRANKIE cannot hear them, she only is aware
of them when they come into her line of view. They instantly
see that the house has been ransacked and they search
desperately through the trunk and discover the theft quickly.*

Ooh. Remembering things coming in now. Oh, nice. Oh,
remembering. Jumping into the water in the old body. Young
body. Splash! Cold, exciting water. The man splashing about
reaching out his hand to me. 'Come on, girl! Swim to me!
Swim to Da, Frannie! Swim to your da! I've got you,
Frannie!' Water plashing round my ears, bright sun blinding
my eyes making bright flashes on the surface. Glitter!
Sequins on the top of the water! Flash! Da's arms. Reaching
out. Head under the water now. Brrrrrm. Pock! Prrrsssssh!
Ears full of sound and then… Head out! Birds shouting!
Swish water! Smiling Da like his smile will crack open his
face. For me! For Frannie! Handsome Da! Holding out his
arms for me!

For me! Reach and flop through the water. Oh, that's
funny! Oh, hahahahahahahaha! Oh, that's so funny! Effort!
Splish! Effort! Splash! Warm hands under my oxters.
Raising me up out of the water! Raised up out of the water
in Daddy's arms!

T-BELLE *rounds on her and shakes her, wanting to know
what has happened.* FRANKIE *is shocked into the present.*

Nasty! Oh, go away! That one. No! Stop at me.

T-BELLE has grabbed the feather fan from FRANKIE's lap and is waving it at her, clearly accusingly. MAY comes into FRANKIE's eyeline and gives the fan back to FRANKIE.

Exactly! That's the way, smiler! That'll show HER. MY thing. Horrible, stupid long-faced moanybones. HORRIBLE! Well, one thing I'll tell you, I don't like HER! Now. I want some cheese.

Waving to get their attention she drops the fan. Looks to the floor. Looks to the women.

Smiler? Hello?? Hello?

Bit of a problem here? Dropped my new thing? Hello?

FRANKIE waves her good hand about, unseen by the others.

MY THING!!!! IS ON THE FLOOR!!!! THE FLOOR IDIOTS!!!! Hey, smiler! My nice new thing??? Stupid idiots! Stupid! Stupid! Stupid! Stupid! Me! Sitting here! Wants the THING! My new white feathery thing!!!!!! Oh, for crying out – Show her with my hands. Wave my hands. I WANT THE… Oh, for the love of – She can't see me. STOP DISTRACTING HER! Nasty old long-face. STOP IT, YOU TWO! PAY ATTENTION TO ME!!!!

She looks once more disconsolately at the floor where the fan has fallen. Trying to figure out a plan.

Now if I could just think.

T-BELLE leaves. MAY goes to follow her, out of FRANKIE's eyeline. Then turns back to notice FRANKIE, looking thoughtfully at the floor. She comes over to her, picks up the fan, to the delighted, wide, active smile of FRANKIE, which MAY mirrors. Then she kisses her on the forehead and goes to leave.

DID IT! I GOT IT BACK! Knew I could! Now. Now what?

Looks up and sees MAY, who has turned back to her. Lights change to the harsh glare of earlier, when FRANKIE was haunted by MAY's look at the threshold of the scene of the 'rape'. FRANKIE looks frozen. The white noise gets louder.

The fizzing gets louder. And new to the soundtrack is the sound of lovemaking, but harsh and frightening.

Don't look at me like that. Don't look at me. Don't look at me, May. Smiler. May.

Scene Seven

The lovemaking soundtrack reaches its climax, and FRANKIE *(live – not on the soundtrack) screams/howls 'Nnnggghaaah!' as if to drown it out and exorcise the noise. Through this, the lights are darkening to night. Wind outside howling. At the climax of sound and scream it all suddenly stops with a slight fizzing sound and then… Silence. The rising of the wind brings us back to the present.* FRANKIE *looks exhausted and blanker than ever. Stillness for a moment.*

The door slams open, flurry of snow and louder wind, and T-BELLE *races in, in a state of extreme agitation and excitement.* FRANKIE *watches listlessly.* T-BELLE *races to the stove and warms herself whilst breathing deeply and perversely removing her muffler and letting her coat fall. She is wearing a loose white garment that leaves her shoulders exposed. She is hectic and flushed with excitement. Vehement.*

T-BELLE. I DID IT! *I DID IT! I DID IT!*

She paces up and down, body alive, furious and pumping like a fighter after a victory. Speaking to FRANKIE *as if she knows she can hear her.*

I didn't know what you meant. I had no notion of what you were talking about but my God! Nelly… Gone… May looked so sick. I wasn't able to… I got so mad… Jed was… He said the money would be forfeit. The bastard! If I'd had the knife I would have… He was. He said we'd have to. He. The musicians were packing up. I was so MAD, Frankie! I was fit to be tied. Fuck him. *Fuck him!*

I said PLAY! I said. He said no point. I said PLAY THE
GODDAMNED TUNE! DO THE LIGHTS! PLAY! PLAY!
PLAY!

I ran onto the stage. I don't know what I was thinking.
Nothing! I was a blank. I crawled into the back of Liberty
and I threw off my clothes. *Ripped them off me*. It was dark.
There was no music. I didn't care, Frankie! I didn't CARE!

She dives on her knees in front of FRANKIE, *who regards
her blankly*.

I started to dance! I started to move. I threw myself from
one steel strut to another. Look! *I've bruised my whole body!*
It was... It was like breathing for the first breath. I heard the
musicians start up. There was a bang. A bang of the lights
fizzing up.

Lights pick out T-BELLE. *We are in the Statue of Liberty
with her now*.

Bam! Oh, I felt it on my face! The heat. On my body, my bare
flesh. I couldn't see a thing. I flailed about inside and I felt
ALIVE! The music was in my head and I crashed my body
from strut to strut and I shouted out at the top of my lungs!

LA PRALINE EN DÉLIRE!

THE DARK GARDEN!

THE HILL OF SEDGE!

HOCHITE WALLUNG!

THE FURY OF LOVE! THE FURY OF LOVE! THE FURY
OF LOVE!

During this, MAY *has entered. She watches* T-BELLE *and*
FRANKIE.

T-BELLE *throws herself flat on the floor in front of*
FRANKIE, *laughing and crying, until she wears herself out.*
FRANKIE, *through the noise of* T-BELLE's *dance, has
started shuddering violently. By the time* T-BELLE *has
finished, it is clear that* FRANKIE *is considerably weakened.*

Did you see me, Mamma? Did you see me dance?

MAY. I saw you.

T-BELLE. Did they cheer? Did they say 'Brava'!?! (*Laughing.*)
Or did they boo me? Did they throw tomatoes? Did they,
Mamma?

MAY. No they didn't.

T-BELLE. And Jed gave us the money?

MAY (*only the slightest pause*). He did.

> T-BELLE *arches back, tired and exhilarated.*

I didn't know where you ran off to.

T-BELLE. I thought I'd run all the way up the pass to... But I
came back... Let's leave tomorrow.

MAY. I think so. You should go to bed. You're tired.

T-BELLE. I suppose we'll have to take her with us.

MAY. I expect we will.

T-BELLE. No. Can't very well leave her here I suppose.

MAY. Go to bed, Tee.

> *She leaves.*

(*Tidies away* T-BELLE*'s things as she speaks.*) You should
have seen her. Somebody should have. There was no one there.

Nelly cut and run. Went off on a boat this afternoon. Like
almost everyone else. The hall was empty. Just two of the
musicians and Jed. They were packing up. I don't know what
demon was in her but Christ, Frankie – excuse my language
– you should have seen her. Jed couldn't take his eyes off
her. He shot the lights up. I didn't recognise her. She was...
another woman.

She ran off after, so she doesn't even know there was no one
there. This is an evil world, Frankie. That... bastard Jed.
Sorry. Language. Oh! I don't care! That poisonous bastard.
He's stolen our money. He said it was the law of the jungle.

He was that cold. It was only after T-Belle danced that he gave me these.

She takes something from her pocket. It is three large-sheet tickets.

Passage. Out of the goodness of his heart he said. He wouldn't see us stuck.

FRANKIE *arches her neck, mouth open.*

Frankie.

Goes to her.

I have a secret. I have a secret to tell you.

That man. T-Belle's daddy...

I'd seen him looking at me, you see. That man you thought you sold me to.

Oh, you had a penny dreadful in your heart when you thought old Junius Brutus saw me and wanted to ravish me against my will.

When I went in to couple with him, Frankie, I turned to you at the door and I had *one* thought in my head, God forgive me. One thought: *Now we're even.* The debt is paid. You saved my life on that ship and I *hated* you for it. Hated that I owed you for ever. But now we were even, because you thought you had done the worst thing a woman could ever do. No one wants to be grateful all their life, Frankie, not even me.

But you know what, my darling? I was in *ecstasy*! *Fevered* with excitement because I'd been waiting for so long. All those nights he'd visit you in your dressing room. From his first half-look to me when I was sewing up your Mopsa dress. I saw it for the first time in my life: *desire*. For me. Not you. *Me!* And I watched you watching him. I know you so well. The more desperate you got for that part I started to have this mean, beautiful thought.

I knew your ambition would stop nowhere, Frankie, I knew you would sacrifice me to him if you could and I wanted... God forgive me, I wanted both. I wanted the debt to be cancelled and I wanted the man too.

So I made it happen. Worked on him like a piece of bobbin lace, thread by thread. It came so easy because *I* desired it too. Just that. That's powerful as a disease. Desire. Powerful as hunger. Sure, he was only a man after all.

You owe me nothing, Frankie.

By the end of this speech it is clear that FRANKIE *has died.* MAY *looks at her for a moment and then settles her shawl around her as if to keep her warm.*

The lights change, and MAY *and* T-BELLE *walk forward to the front of the stage. Cold daytime light. Wind and creaking boat noises above the just-audible sound of the music box.*

I did a strange thing then. I took Frankie out into the snow, T-Belle was still asleep, exhausted I suppose. I laid Frankie out with her good arm raised above her head and I went back to the warm house and I slept. The next morning I went out to where I had laid Frankie out. She was stiff and cold like I knew she'd be, just as I had left her. I couldn't think how I would find the strength to do what I wanted to do, but then I heard a person approaching me and when I turned to look it was an Indian man and he said, in his halting English, that his name was Joe. Somehow I felt that I could trust him so I told him what I wanted to do and he did it.

Then I went back and I woke T-Belle and I told her that Frankie was dead and that we had to go. She didn't ask me anything, but just packed up the things and followed me, and we made our way to the rackety little ship with our boxes and our little few things. T-Belle was dazed, like a person in a trance, and when we got to the ship I turned her gently and I showed her what the Indian man and I had done. She looked over to the Statue of Liberty I had made, all the lace I had saved from the old days draped over Frankie, and she raised up in her stiffness against the shack, just visible from the dock, the lace torn and fluttering now from our efforts, and she saw Frankie standing upright, her arm raised up like she was carrying a torch. T-Belle didn't change the frozen look on her face, just hefted the boxes onto the boat. All the others turned away as well.

And like dirty words had been spoken, the little ship set off
with not one person looking back at my Frankie, my friend.

T-BELLE. We stood on the deck, Mamma and me, and we didn't
stand too close. I saw the mountains, beautiful in a way I had
not seen since we first saw them. And below I saw the strand,
churned up with slush and the filth from our animals and our
dirty sleds. We had churned up the whole strip from the base
of the mountains to the shore. As the boat rounded the
headland away from Dyea I turned away and looked out to
sea. It was then that I heard May, speaking softly:

MAY.
    'Music; awake her: strike!
    'Tis time: descend: be stone no more: approach:
    Strike all that look upon with marble.'

T-BELLE (*slight irritation*). Marvel.

MAY (*slight irritation*). Marvel.

    (*Composes herself for the solemnity of the moment.*)
                    'Come,
    I'll fill your grave up. Stir. Nay, come away.
    Bequeath to death your numbness, for from him
    Dear life redeems you. – You perceive she stirs…'

T-BELLE. And I turned and looked. But I was tardy as ever. A
fluttering of lace was all I managed to see before the boat
rounded the headland and headed out to the open sea.

The End.

A Nick Hern Book

In Skagway first published in Great Britain in 2014 as a paperback original by Nick Hern Books Limited, The Glasshouse, 49a Goldhawk Road, London W12 8QP, in association with KTR Productions

In Skagway copyright © 2014 Karen Ardiff

Karen Ardiff has asserted her moral right to be identified as the author of this work

Cover photography by Bronwen Sharp; image design by Carmen del Prado Cover design by Ned Hoste, 2H

Typeset by Nick Hern Books, London
Printed in Great Britain by Mimeo Ltd, Huntingdon, Cambridgeshire PE29 6XX

A CIP catalogue record for this book is available from the British Library

ISBN   978 1 84842 394 7